A brilliant step-by-step guide t
want and buy! It's one thing to w
work for your business. Karen h
what you need to do from gettir
a buzz and helping it position yc

Fiona Harrold, bestselling author, *Be Your Own Life Coach*

I found Karen's wisdom in *Book Marketing Made Simple* invaluable when I was writing my first book. Like many aspiring authors I was focused on writing my book rather than marketing it and although by the time I picked up Karen's book and attended her 30 Day Challenge most of my writing was done, I was able to use her amazing advice in organising and delivering a book launch I could be proud of.

As Karen emphasises in this revised 2nd edition, marketing your book is an ongoing process and I have been eagerly awaiting her revised words of wisdom so I can put them into practice, and I am now brimming with ideas to keep publicising my book.

I love Karen's willingness to experiment and to try new things. Just reading her story, and those of people she has interviewed in the book, is an inspiration. Karen's book is full of ideas and recommendations, without being overwhelming. She writes with authority and in an engaging manner, which makes this book a page-turner and one to keep coming back to. I can't wait to put all her wisdom into practice for my next book!

Katie Conley, career coach and author of *God's GRACE for Your Career: Rediscover Your Purpose at Work*

Book Marketing Made Simple is a treasure trove of invaluable advice for authors and business owners alike. As someone who wrote and published my first book recently to complement my business and help build authority, Karen's expertise in the first edition was a game-changer. Now, with the new edition, I've gained even more valuable tips for marketing and writing future books. From suggestions around ISBNs to creative ways to use your book to grow your business, to information on alternative formats such as e-books and audio to even video, TV and radio promotion,

Karen's real-life examples and industry insights make this a must-have book for both budding and experienced authors. It's the go-to reference I'll keep coming back to. Highly recommended for anyone seeking success in book marketing.

Joanne Moorhouse, author of *Remote Stories Around the World* and Creative Director of Joanne Moorhouse Photography

I wish I knew all this before I started writing! 27 books later and barely any sales show that I love writing but really don't know anything about being a BESTSELLING author. What's the point if no one knows my work exists? Karen is an absolute lifesaver and has given me hope that maybe there is a way that I can get my books out there to someone other than my immediate family. *Book Marketing Made Simple* has hit the nail on the head and Karen's wealth of experience will help so many authors or wannabe authors see their work flourish. She offers fantastic advice that makes perfect sense in a practical and easy to follow format. I was hooked from page one and you will be too.

Angela De Souza, Women's Business Club and author of *I Did it in my Pyjamas* and many other unknown books!

Book Marketing Made Simple is jam packed with great nuggets and key steps on everything any author would want to know about marketing their book and more! I like the fact that it is easy to dip in and out of, so that you can read areas that particularly interest you, and it also has some really useful timesaving strategies. The case studies and tips show that Karen knows what she's talking about and how she can help you. It is an all-round good read and excellent book on every aspect to help authors to maximise their marketing opportunities and sell more books!

Steve Preston, The Career Catalyst and author of *Portfolio Careers – How to Work for Passion, Pleasure and Profit!*, *Winning Through Career Change* and *Winning Through Redundancy*

I love this book! From start to finish, it's absolutely crammed full of useful and inspirational advice on how to get the most out of writing and publishing a book, written in an easy to follow, bite-size chunk approach. And having published ten books herself, Karen Williams knows her stuff when it comes to book-aligned marketing. This is a step-by-step guide on how to build a successful business with a book as a core marketing strategy. It definitely over delivers, which is a nice change from a lot of other books out there on the same subject by authors who just use their book to lead you into their expensive programmes. Karen's book openly and generously shares detailed knowledge covering every aspect of creating a book that is in alignment with your business and a business that is in alignment with your book!

In addition to the tips and useful 'things to think about' summaries, Karen uses her own and her clients' experiences to give useful real-life examples of strategies that have worked or not worked and this is invaluable. She even offers some useful free resources via a special website link.

Whether you are a new or experienced author, or maybe even just started out and haven't yet written a word, this book will help you align and leverage your efforts to make more impact, sell more books, help more people and ultimately grow your business. And that's something we all need.

Having published my first book with little knowledge of the industry and no real plan for its marketing other than my own raw enthusiasm, I'm delighted to have this book by my side as I prepare to launch my next. A definitive guide that will pay for itself a thousand times over.

Ellen Watts, author of *Cosmic Ordering Made Easier: How to get more of what you want – more often* and *Get it Sorted – for once, for all, for GOOD*

Writing a book is only part of the challenge, selling it is another and each requires very different skills and knowledge sets. In her book, Karen clearly demonstrates the huge range of marketing opportunities that begin even before putting pen to paper. Your challenge after reading this book will no longer be how to market your book, but more, which of these great methods to choose. An invaluable practical guide to marketing your masterpiece.

Louise Wiles, co-author of *Thriving Abroad: The Definitive Guide to Professional and Personal Relocation Success* and co-host of the podcast Successful Student Transitions

Writing a book is challenging, marketing it, even more so. Putting yourself and your book out there can be a big step outside your comfort zone for many people; it was for me! And yet why go to the bother of writing a book to build your business in order to help more people, and then do nothing with it ... Here you will gain Karen's valuable insight (and those of other experts), gaining access to some very clever ways to market your book and your business. Furthermore, there is a choice of strategies to suit your personality and preferred communication methods. As a finance coach, I have seen many businesses spend enormous amounts of money on their marketing, all on fruitless strategies. Here you will get some great strategies whilst saving a fortune too. As an author, I can testify that the strategies do work. Furthermore, as an accountant I can testify to the savings too. They are all great value for money! The only thing left for you to do is choose the ones you want to do and then go do them.

Helen Monaghan, HM Finance Coaching & Advisory Ltd, and author of *Successful Business Minds*, *The Magical Mix of Money & Tax*, and *12 Steps to Improve Your Cashflow*

I was fortunate enough to peer review the draft of this book. Having worked with Karen to get my first book published, some of it was familiar. But obviously, no matter how much time you spend with someone they cannot articulate all of their wisdom. This book is just packed with valuable nuggets. I found myself compelled to methodically go through step by step to ensure I had truly maximised my potential to market my book. Guess what? I hadn't. There is so much knowledge and wisdom shared in this book not only from Karen but other marketing experts that I found myself able to not only learn new things but also improve current processes. This will definitely become one of those books with the pages written all over and completely bent backwards as it will be with me every step of the way with all my future marketing activity. Thank you Karen.

Sheryl Andrews, Step by Step Listening and author of *Manage your Critic – From Overwhelm to Clarity in 7 Steps*

Karen has written a book that works. It is a great read, with many case studies and stories, and at the same time is a supremely practical guide to the whole process of marketing a book. Starting with the very first glimmer of your idea – through writing, promoting, funding, and publishing – with detailed guidance all the way, this book comes highly recommended.

Mary Lunnen, Dare to Blossom Life Coaching and author of six books including *The Powerful Voice of the Quiet Ones* and *Your Compass Rose Speaks: Rediscover Your Inner Wisdom*

Some superb hints and tips contained within the book that I will use for marketing my own book. Help to navigate the social media minefields was just what I needed, and information about Goodreads was new to me. I loved the detailed tips for the physical launch party, and the other options of a virtual launch, or an Amazon bestseller launch, were intriguing options. I am already implementing the advice and reaping the rewards, thank you!

Jane Langston, co-author of *Muscle Testing: A Concise Manual*

BOOK MARKETING MADE SIMPLE

Revised & Expanded 2nd Edition

Practical Steps to Generate Sales, Opportunities, and Clients as You Write and Launch Your Business Book

KAREN WILLIAMS

Printed in the United Kingdom
First Printing, 2017
Second Printing, 2023

ISBN 978-1-7395064-0-7 (Print)
ISBN 978-1-7395064-1-4 (eBook)

Librotas Books
Portsmouth Hampshire
PO2 9NT

www.LibrotasBooks.com

Contents

SECTION 3: POST-LAUNCH PROMOTION   **223**

Acknowledgements

I want to express my gratitude to the experts I have had the privilege of learning from since I started out in business in 2006. These include the successful coaches I interviewed for my first book in 2009, as well as the coaches, mentors, and trainers who have generously shared their knowledge and provided inspiration. Thank you for shaping my learning and for your unwavering support.

I owe a great deal to my clients who have entrusted me with their aspirations of raising their profile and becoming authorities in their fields. Your unique perspectives and experiences have taught me invaluable lessons in book marketing. I am thrilled to showcase many of your stories within the pages of this book. Thank you for your trust and collaboration.

I would like to extend my heartfelt appreciation to my team, without whom I couldn't produce multiple books and support our clients: Tracy Harris, Sheryl Andrews, Mark Edmunds, and Brenna McNeill. And my publishing team: Louise Lubke Cuss and Samantha Pearce.

Additionally, I'd like to thank everyone else involved in the creation of this book. I would like to acknowledge the experts and contributors who have graciously shared their expertise and perspectives and I highly recommend you listen to these remarkable individuals on your journey: Steve Bimpson, Ginny Carter, Steve Randall, Alison Colley, Alice Fewings, Karen Duncan, Caroline Andrew-Johnstone, Ellen Watts, Helen McCusker, Samantha Pearce, Elliott Frisby, Dielle Hannah, and Naomi Jane Johnson. And thanks to those who have already told me how much they love the book and for your praise,

Karen Skidmore for kindly writing the foreword, and everyone who has helped me to promote it.

Thank you to my family and friends for your patience, understanding, and unwavering support throughout the process of writing and reviewing this book. Your belief in me and the time you have given me have been truly invaluable.

And lastly, I would like to extend my gratitude to you, the reader, for embarking on this journey with me and for investing your time and energy into your own book. May the insights and strategies in these pages inspire you to achieve the remarkable success you truly deserve.

Foreword

I have birthed many things over the years, from online courses and groundbreaking programmes to two books and two children. Undoubtedly the toughest births were both my books, yet, despite the challenges, would I embark on writing another one? Absolutely! And I have my third one bubbling up inside of me as I write this.

My first book, *Shiny Shiny: How to Stop Being a Social Media Magpie*, came out at the start of 2004. It began life as a 10,000 word e-book and after much talking and not much doing, I was challenged by a good friend at the time to 'shut up and get on with it' so it could become a fully-fledged paperback book. I decided to sprint it and six weeks later, I had brought together 200+ articles from my blog, reorganised and rewritten them and ta dah ... my first book was completed.

I self-published it and I was very proud of it, but boy did I make some major mistakes. You see, even as a business coach and marketer at the time, I hadn't really thought out how I would use this book to build my business. I focused all my time on the writing of the content and making it look good, and only thought about how to market it once I had a copy in my hands.

My second book, *True Profit Business: How to play your bigger game without burning out*, was published in September 2019. Having learnt my lessons from book number one, I thought through the strategy and marketing of it far more and was delighted when it was shortlisted as a Business Book Awards Finalist in 2020. However, there was so much more I could have done to promote it, especially now having read this book.

This book that you have in your hands right now is an integral part of your book writing and publishing journey. Karen Williams has mapped out everything you need to think about, both pre- and post-book launch, and I love the client stories she shares and how she brings in other experts to contribute and add value to each chapter.

It's too easy to focus only on the writing of a book. Yes, the writing may feel like the most time-consuming part, as well as hugely emotional as you bare your soul, share your expertise and have your truth immortalised forever in print.

And I get that you may not be looking to write a *Sunday Times* Bestseller, but without a well thought out marketing strategy, you are in danger of becoming 'just another author' in a very crowded marketplace. With more than 4 million new books published each year (and these numbers will only increase now we have ChatGPT to churn out content faster than you click your mouse), spending time on your marketing strategy for your book is essential.

So yes, you are embarking on a big journey, and I know I haven't put you off. Because I know from experience when you want to write a book, that drive and passion within you to want to share your expertise with the world will see you through.

And putting things into action from what you read in this book will ensure you have more than just a book ... you will have a book that has the potential of changing the world because the right people will want to seek out and read it. I wish you all the success in the birth of your book.

Karen Skidmore, founder of Grow Strong® and author of *True Profit Business*

INTRODUCTION

CHAPTER 1
Author mistakes and marketing secrets

My first book was a game-changer, as it put me and my business on the map in ways I never anticipated. Prior to the pivotal decision to write it in the summer of 2009, my coaching business was trundling along, attracting new clients here and there, but it lacked the ability to make a real impact – the very reason I became a coach in the first place. However, everything changed when I decided to write and publish a book.

Fast forward 18 arduous months of research, interviews, planning, writing, editing, and re-editing, striving to find the right publisher, and overcoming my inner critic, in March 2011, I stood before an enthusiastic audience of over 70 people at my first book launch. Exhausted but exhilarated, I couldn't help but be delighted with what I had achieved. And that was just the start of my journey.

Now, I wish I could say I had a meticulously crafted marketing plan for *The Secrets of Successful Coaches*. But the truth is, I didn't. Despite my background in business and marketing, my launch was a patchwork of efforts. I lacked a strong plan, essentially throwing everything I had at it and hoping something would stick. Surprisingly, it did!

I credit that book for propelling me and my business into the spotlight. The launch was a resounding success, with my book quickly claiming the Amazon bestseller spot, reaching readers worldwide, and opening the doors to valuable opportunities, partnerships, and joint ventures.

Since then, I've continued to write and publish non-fiction books, refining what works and rejecting what doesn't. I am currently the author of ten entrepreneurial books. These include *Your Book is the Hook*, which takes non-fiction authors through all the steps involved in the book production process, *The Mouse That Roars*, charting my own entrepreneurial journey and, most recently, *The 7 Shifts*, which lays the groundwork for aspiring authors to refine their impactful idea, gain confidence in sharing their stories, and hone the message contained within their expertise.

Since 2014, as The Book Mentor, my team and I have supported hundreds of experts, entrepreneurs, and thought leaders through the whole process of planning, writing, launching, and marketing their own successful non-fiction books and memoirs, some of whom you will meet in upcoming chapters.

Had I possessed this book back in 2009, my journey would have been considerably smoother. I could have saved myself an immense amount of time, frustration, and energy. But then I wouldn't have been able to share my insights, as these challenges prompted my research and learning around these topics. And through this updated second edition, my goal is to simplify the lives of business authors like you across the globe.

Author mistakes

I originally wrote this book in 2017 because there was something that really frustrated me. I saw too many business authors write brilliant books but fail to promote them.

They would pour hours into researching their topic, searching for a unique angle, crafting their framework, and putting their thoughts onto paper. Then they'd approach the difficult process of editing and refining the manuscript until it was perfect.

Meanwhile, they would explore publishing options, whether painstakingly finding an agent or publisher, or venturing into self-publishing or partnership arrangements. Their book would finally be produced, and they would feel the rush of excitement upon receiving those shiny new copies with their name on the front cover.

Whilst all of these elements are essential, it wouldn't be long before those books would sit neglected in cupboards or garages, collecting dust, as the authors failed to promote, market, or sell their masterpieces.

They didn't let anyone know they had written a book, so it became the world's best kept secret – and an expensive business card! It languished on Amazon without any reviews, so it remained unnoticed. They lacked a plan to leverage their book as a tool for marketing and business growth.

I get it. You might feel that once your book is out in the world, the hard work should be over. After investing considerable time and energy into writing it, it's not surprising that you might find yourself running low on steam when it's time to promote it.

And fear may creep in. Even after writing and publishing your book, you might wonder what people will think, if they'll like it, and how to handle negative feedback. But if you never share your wisdom with your ideal audience, how will you ever know?

Marketing secrets

So here is the secret to having a successful book. Marketing it well must be a primary consideration right from the beginning of your writing journey. Not something you should only start considering when your book is in your hands. Especially if you aspire to use your book to build your credibility, stand out, and raise your profile.

That's why this book aims to help you to market your book (and your business) alongside your writing. It is designed to empower you with effective tools and strategies to promote your book, elevate your credibility, and make a lasting impact.

By implementing the ideas shared within these pages at the earliest opportunity, the transition from writing to launch will be seamless. You can generate more income, sell numerous copies, expand your business, and reach and influence a wider audience. Even if you've come across this book later in the process or after your book's launch, you can still benefit from the advice contained within. However, you may need to tailor your approach more specifically.

This book is primarily for business owners who are publishing a physical book and may also produce an e-book and audiobook alongside it. However, it's important to note that many of these strategies can also be applied to those who are solely producing e-books (and fiction writers may benefit from some of the ideas).

Your book may take the form of a manual, textbook, how-to guide, self-help book, anthology, parable, memoir, or any other type that serves as a marketing tool and credibility builder. It's crucial to approach your writing with a business mindset. The strategies presented in this book will empower you to maximise the value of your hard work, knowledge, and writing, ultimately helping you grow your business through the power of your book.

There are lots of marketing strategies within this book. You may be familiar with, and perhaps using, some of these already. If they are working for you, please continue with these approaches and make tweaks if you learn something new. As for the additional marketing activities that you are not already doing, choose those that resonate with you, that you will enjoy doing, and that will help you reach your ideal clients and readers.

Pursuing speaking engagements won't be fruitful if the thought terrifies you. Building an online community won't yield results if you're technologically averse or unwilling to outsource such tasks, especially if you know you'll struggle to maintain regular contact. However, sometimes you need to push past your comfort zone and tackle the things that scare you. Don't let fear be an excuse.

Ultimately, select the strategies that you instinctively know will benefit you and commit to them consistently. Initially, you might start with a handful of strategies, but as your business and book evolve, you will probably integrate, streamline, and automate your marketing, making implementation simpler. In due course, you may delegate some of the initial strategies you have previously handled personally, allowing you to focus on what you do best, which is likely the expertise you share in your book.

I encourage you to adopt a multi-pronged approach, combining offline and online strategies consistently to achieve the most effective results. Stay committed to your marketing efforts, measure the outcomes, fine-tune your activities, and reap the rewards of your investment in your book. As you'll discover in the following chapters, many of the benefits will stem from the products, services, and other offerings you create from your book's foundation.

Why have I created a second edition and why now?

This second edition has been revised and updated for many reasons. The world has undergone significant changes since 2017 when this book was originally published. Whilst the fundamental principles of book marketing remain unchanged, such as understanding your customers' needs, crafting a clear message, and leveraging your book to showcase your expertise, the methods and tactics for implementing these principles have evolved hugely.

The rise in self-publishing has brought about a seismic shift, enabling anyone to write and publish a book with minimal experience. However, as more entrepreneurs recognise the value of authorship in establishing authority, it's not enough to produce a great book; you must also adopt innovative marketing approaches. And even if you secure a publishing deal, most publishers now require a substantial following before commissioning a book.

Digital media, technological advancements, and artificial intelligence (AI) are progressing at a rapid pace, necessitating our continuous adaptation to new strategies that facilitate writing and promotion. There are specific book-related marketing tools available that can simplify the process for authors, but awareness of their existence and how to effectively use them is crucial.

Trends are also shifting. Social media has now become an essential tool for book promotion. Video content and podcasts have gained popularity as effective means to cut through the noise and emotionally engage with audiences while delivering concise messages. And Google Ads and social media advertising have emerged as powerful tools, allowing authors to reach specific demographics and tailor their messaging to resonate with potential readers.

Although these tools can be powerful for reaching new audiences, expanding your following, and connecting with prospects, it's equally vital to build your own community, create partnerships, and develop marketing collateral that facilitates meaningful relationships with your readers.

In addition to these changes, we have navigated the challenges posed by the COVID-19 pandemic, forcing authors to adapt their book marketing strategies to an increasingly online world. The pandemic has necessitated new methods of marketing, launching, and delivering books. Furthermore, with increased leisure time, many individuals seized this period as an opportunity to write and publish their own books, so there is more competition for readers.

My business has also evolved since 2017. I have gathered more amazing success stories from clients who have achieved incredible results in marketing their books. I wanted to explore expert tips that align with evolving business directions and strategies and showcase some of the people I have worked with during this period. And let's face it, the more books I write, the more my voice continues to develop.

As a result, the entire book has undergone a comprehensive refresh and update. Most chapters contain new content. There's a new chapter dedicated to reviews, endorsements and creating your 'street team' to support your book launch. There's extensive information on ensuring your book is found online. The social media chapter has been revamped, and there's expanded information on list building, creating funnels, online networking and speaking, podcast strategies, audiobook production, creating collaborations, and some new and exciting visibility tactics that some of my clients have been using.

I know I've mentioned this already; however, I really must emphasise the benefits of book marketing right from the moment you start writing – if not before! In my signature programme, the Smart Author System, which launched in April 2020, I focus on using your book writing time to self-fund the process. This approach offers two key advantages: you can reap the rewards of your work from the very start as people get to know you and your expertise, and you have the luxury of time to craft a truly exceptional book without rushing the process. Both of these can produce welcome benefits in a difficult business landscape where money and time can be sparse. I will touch on this throughout the book, so you can see how it works in practice.

I want to ensure that when you write your book, it is aligned with your business, as this is where you'll achieve the best results. All the book marketing and promotion strategies I'll share with you work most effectively when they are intricately linked to your business objectives.

Please note that the information in this second edition is correct at the time of publication, but marketing changes ever so quickly, so bear with me if something evolves and changes! For example, whilst undertaking the final edits of this book, Twitter was in the process of rebranding to X, so feel free to use 'X' rather than 'Twitter' as you work your way through the book, although it will always be Twitter to me!

Also, I approach this book as a book mentor rather than a marketer. My goal is to provide you with ideas and inspiration, guiding you through the entire book process, not just the marketing aspect. I also encourage you to seek additional support from experts in specific areas where you require further information. Together, we can simplify and demystify the important world of marketing, making it more accessible and manageable!

How to get started with this book

If you're wondering where to start, I've organised this book into three main sections. Before diving into the first part, I'll provide you with an introduction to what you should have in place before embarking on your book marketing journey – ideally even before you start writing your book.

Then, I'll guide you through how and when to market your book when you reach the three key milestones: pre-launch, launch, and post-launch.

Pre-launch: This phase encompasses the beginning of your book writing journey leading up to your book's launch. As I mentioned earlier, you may already be implementing some of the suggestions in your business, while others may be new ideas you've considered but weren't sure how to approach. Many of these strategies will continue to be valuable for your ongoing business marketing as well as promoting your book, even after you've launched it.

Launch: I'll share specific actions you can take to successfully launch your book. Some of these approaches require planning, so don't wait until your actual launch date to implement them. These include promoting your book on Amazon, becoming a bestseller, hosting a launch party, and attracting publicity.

Post-launch: It's crucial to maintain momentum after publishing your book, yet many people overlook the importance of ongoing promotion. I'll provide you with strategies to continue spreading the word about your book and how it can benefit readers.

If you're in the early stages of writing your book, I recommend reading this entire book now. You'll gain insight into tasks you'll focus on later, even if you revisit these specific sections when you reach those stages.

If you're further along in your writing journey, I still encourage you to read the entire book, as there are valuable tips applicable to all stages that you can integrate as you see fit.

In this book, I'll be sharing some of my own secrets and strategies, alongside stories and advice from others. My aim is to provide practical ideas that you can implement without consuming too much of your time, by being smart about the process.

Occasionally, I may reference additional resources available on my website, as it's impossible to include everything within these pages. Feel free to review those resources, as they'll complement the information you'll find in this book.

To complement this book, I have also produced the *Book Marketing Planner*. This provides you with space to record your insights as you are inspired by the ideas and gives you a structured place to create your own marketing plan. To get your copy of the planner, go to www.librotas.com/bookmarketingplanner.

Before we dive into the strategies, I want to extend an invitation. If you'd like personalised support throughout the book process – from planning to writing, launching, and marketing – my team and I are here to assist you. You can visit www.librotas.com to learn more or email karen@librotas.com.

Now, let's get started!

CHAPTER 2
Motivation, market, message, and media

As an author, it is essential you have a clear and confident understanding of what your book is about and how it can positively impact your readers' lives. Although this may be obvious, what would you say when someone asks about your book? Could you tell them who your book is for, what it aims to achieve, and how it can truly help people?

Being clear on your book's purpose is crucial in generating excitement and anticipation among potential readers. Unfortunately, many authors struggle to effectively articulate their book's message, which can result in disengaged audiences and missed opportunities for effectively conveying valuable insights and solutions.

However, when you have clarity in your book's message, you will be clear on what content you might share in your blog. You will be confidently developing your social media messages. If you are pitching to a publisher, you can write your synopsis and prepare a compelling proposal. It will make your book easier to write and it will give you the confidence to contact influential people for reviews and testimonials. You will know which podcasts you need to feature on, what publications you want to target, and what videos you need to create. You get the picture!

To embark on this journey, let's begin, in this chapter, by clarifying your vision, motivation, and goals for your book.

Motivation

Having a clear understanding of your desired outcomes is crucial for measuring and achieving success with your book. Whether your aspirations are personal or business related, defining your vision and establishing specific goals is the first step toward realising them.

In my Smart Author System, getting clarity on your vision forms the initial stage of the 'Starting with the end in mind' section. Because without a clear destination in mind, you can't navigate your journey or gauge your progress.

It is likely that you have a personal vision, such as changing lives, sharing your lessons, and leaving a legacy. I expect you have a business vision, which may include more tangible outcomes such as building your business, gaining more clients, and creating new opportunities, and you also are likely to have compelling reasons for taking the steps to write it. Additionally, you may have specific goals tied to your book, such as a target date for its publication.

I invite you now to consider your goals and vision for this book, so they are crystal clear. It will lay solid foundations by clarifying your aspirations, so you are motivated and confident to take the next steps in your journey.

After vision, the next thing I cover with clients in this area is what I call alignment and leverage. Aligning everything that you do in your business (by being clear on what you do and who you do it for) will allow you to leverage your knowledge through your book (allowing you to multiply the outcome of your efforts without a corresponding increase in resources). Let's explore this topic further with some practical steps you can take.

Market, message, and media

You may have heard of the concept Market, Message, and Media, which traditionally applies to marketing and communication, and it can equally apply to your book's success. By focusing on these aspects at an early stage, you'll be equipped to connect with your ideal readers, effectively communicate your unique message, and strategically promote your book through the right channels.

Your market: Who are your ideal readers and clients? Understanding your target audience is crucial for effective book marketing. By identifying and defining your market, you can tailor your messaging, content, and promotional activities to resonate with their needs, desires, and aspirations. Niche targeting allows you to reach the right people who are most likely to connect with your book's message and become enthusiastic advocates for your work.

Your message: What sets your book apart? What problem does it solve, or what valuable insights does it offer? Your message encapsulates the unique value proposition of your book and forms the core of your marketing communication. It is the essence of what you want to convey to your target audience. By refining and articulating your message, you can effectively capture the attention and interest of potential readers.

Your media: How will you deliver your message to your target audience? Media refers to the channels and platforms through which you will reach and engage your readers. This can include your website, social media platforms, email marketing, speaking engagements, podcast appearances, and more. By selecting the most appropriate media channels for your specific audience, you can effectively distribute and amplify your message, expanding your book's reach and impact.

I'll cover your market and message in this chapter to set the scene, and media will be covered throughout the book.

Market: understanding your readers

Your market consists of the individuals who are most likely to read and consume your book. It is crucial to write a book that resonates with your target audience, attracting the very people you love working with in your business. In fact, your ideal reader is often your ideal client. Therefore, it's essential to align your book's topic and content with your existing audience unless you intend to diversify your business or venture into a new niche.

One common mistake I see when authors write their books is the misconception that broader content will attract a larger audience. However, the most successful books for building a business are those that specifically target a particular group of people.

If you believe your book can help anyone with anything, or if you are unsure about who your ideal reader is, it's important to revisit and clarify this aspect before completing your book (ideally, even before starting it). Defining your ideal reader is crucial because it fundamentally impacts both your book and its marketing strategy.

Remember, your book is your chance to position yourself as an expert, and use it as an effective marketing tool, so you may choose to niche quite deeply in your book. For example, *Book Marketing Made Simple* will only attract a limited part of the entire population, but it will help business authors who want to make money from their book, and use it as a business-building strategy. And it's amazing how many businesspeople actually want to do this!

Ultimately you want to create a book – and a business – that allows you to play to your strengths and hit your sweet spot. This is the place where you can do what you love, do what you're good at, and ideally get paid well!

Take a moment to review your ideal client and reader, who they are, what their challenges are and what they might want from your book.

Message: refining and defining your book's purpose

When you have a clear understanding of your ideal reader, it becomes easier to define the topic of your book, create its content, and plan your marketing efforts. This clarity also enables you to develop a compelling message that effectively communicates the problem you're solving or the new information you're providing to your readers – perhaps even both! However, it's important to note that your book should focus on a specific topic rather than trying to include everything you know. If you have multiple topics to share, consider creating subsequent books that delve into specific areas. Remember, you're not limited to writing just one book.

If you find yourself struggling to articulate your exact message or haven't reached this stage yet, consider conducting a survey or interviews with your clients and prospects. These self-funding and self-validating techniques that I teach in the Smart Author System can provide valuable insights.

Even if you believe you know your book's focus, validating your ideas with your target audience can ensure you're on the right track. Additionally, these techniques can raise your profile and may even lead to client interest and engagement with your services while you're still in the process of writing your book. For more information about the Smart Author System, you can visit www.librotas.com/smart-author.

This market research will give you deeper insights into your clients' biggest struggles, goals, aspirations, and the obstacles hindering their process. This research can yield both qualitative and quantitative responses, providing statistical data that highlights key areas you need to address and captures the exact words your clients use, which can be used in your copy and marketing materials.

If you're contemplating whether to conduct interviews or surveys, consider using both methods. Surveys offer the advantage of building your email list, while interviews provide an excellent opportunity to reconnect with previous clients and potentially connect with new ones. As an example, one of my clients used interviews a few years ago and generated £5,000 in new business, illustrating the self-funding aspect of this approach. Here is another inspiring example of a client who successfully used surveys in her business.

CLIENT STORY
Lorraine Palmer
author of *Raw Food in a Flash*

When Lorraine came to me to get help to write her book, she was using her book to niche in a smaller market than she was working in already. Although she worked in the raw food sphere, she wanted to use her book to position herself as the go-to person supporting ladies going through the menopause through the medium of eating a diet consisting of mainly raw food.

One of the reasons why she decided to niche in this area was that she had gone through early menopause herself, and raw food was the thing that helped her to get through it. She wanted to use these experiences to help others.

Due to the fact that Lorraine was using her book to reposition herself as an expert in a niched area, I suggested she carry out a survey as part of the research for her book.

She used Surveymonkey.com to carry out a survey to find out what people were struggling with and where they needed support.

This survey resulted in over 100 people who couldn't wait to receive her book. With their permission, Lorraine added these ladies to her mailing list so that she could keep in touch with them as she was writing it.

If you'd like to carry out a survey for your book, you can download my 'How-to guide' at www.librotas.com/free.

Your angle and hook

It's important that your message doesn't sound like everyone else's. Given that there may be numerous resources and books already available on your chosen topic, consider your unique angle and hook. This concept is introduced in my third book, *Your Book is the Hook*. Your angle represents your distinctive perspective or approach to a subject, while your hook is the attention-grabbing element that captivates people's interest.

Your angle can be shaped by the type of person you are writing for – specifically, the particular group of individuals who are your ideal readers. Your hook, on the other hand, revolves around the problem you are addressing for these individuals. What sets your book apart is the unique way in which you position yourself, tackle the problem, and provide a solution.

Closely linked to your message is what you want to be known for in your industry or niche. It's important to convey this effectively in your book. Let me share with you another client example to illustrate this concept further.

🗐 CLIENT STORY
Jenny Phillips
author of *Eat to OUTSMART Cancer*

Jenny Phillips published her first book, *Eat to OUTSMART Cancer*, in 2015. I helped her to write the book and develop her message. The motivation behind Jenny's business as a nutritionist was that she went into this profession after using nutrition in her own bid to overcome breast cancer when she was 39.

After many years practising as a nutritionist, she found that she worked with many patients who were going through a similar experience, or wanted to improve their health to avoid cancer.

With each patient she saw, she found she was saying the same thing. That's why she wrote her book: to get this message to more people who needed to hear it.

The angle that she took was having her book specifically aimed towards those going through cancer and those who wished to avoid the disease.

Her hook was the positive results that she and her clients were getting from following her programme.

This helped her to raise her profile, and while she was writing her book, Jenny was approached to run nutrition events for a cancer charity, and that was before she'd even finished and published it!

In the process of discovering your unique angle or hook, I would like to offer you another valuable piece of advice. Take the time to research and explore what has already been written and published in your area of expertise. By doing so, you can gain a deeper understanding of your competition and identify what sets you and your book apart.

Your story: drawing from personal experience

The topic and content of your book may be rooted in your own story – how your experiences have shaped the person you are today and what you aim to convey in your book. You've already heard about two of my clients: Jenny, whose life took a new direction after battling breast cancer, and Lorraine, who transformed her business following an early menopause. Their personal experiences influenced the books they wrote and the niche markets they support.

It's essential to gain clarity on why you are the best person to write this book. Understand how your knowledge and expertise make you an authority in your field. Recognise how your unique journey has brought you to where you are today. These elements will help you write your book with authenticity and vulnerability. Additionally, be willing to share your own story within your book, as it has the power to inspire and resonate with your readers.

I must acknowledge that sharing your story may not always be easy. It may require digging deep and summoning bravery to open up about your journey. Here's another example from a client to illustrate the transformative impact of embracing vulnerability and sharing personal experiences within a book.

CLIENT STORY
Rochelle Bugg
author of *Handle With Care*

In 2012, Rochelle Bugg nursed her mum, who had a brain tumour, and blogged about the experience. As a carer in her twenties, there wasn't much support available for her and her two sisters, and her dad had sadly passed away ten years earlier. She wrote her blog to keep her sane, share her thoughts, and help others in a similar situation.

To reach more people and make a bigger difference, in 2016 she decided to turn her blog into a book to help people through her story and her journey, and ensure that other people don't have to go through the same tough times. Her goal is to inspire other young carers and give them the tools that she didn't have when she needed them.

This is what she told me:

"The book helped me to get clear on the value of what I have to offer. I've found that writing a book is a great resource when it comes to social media content. I think it's important to remember what a rich source of 'readymade' content a book gives you. You can pick out quotes to make into memes but also have themes that you can pick for longer posts and newsletter content. For example, I've tweaked content from my book as the basis to write articles for big international lifestyle websites. The content that you write in your book is really versatile and can be repackaged in so many ways – articles for third parties, speaking engagements, and a framework for an e-course.

"I think there's a certain kudos and automatic respect that comes from having written a book on a specific subject. It's great at helping to establish yourself within an industry and sets you apart from the competition. Even being able to write a press release and quote yourself as 'published author of book XYZ' is so much stronger and more likely to be picked up.

"The book writing process has also helped to build my confidence – it's reassured me that I have a body of knowledge and experience to share, as well as helping me get clear on my areas of expertise. In turn that will help with marketing when writing press releases, pitching stories to media, and seeking out speaking engagements, as I'm a lot clearer on who I am and my message."

Handle with Care was published by John Blake Books in March 2021. It was serialised in *You Magazine* in the *Mail on Sunday* and Rochelle appeared across a variety of international media and podcasts, including Sky News, BBC News, and *Cosmopolitan*. She has given extensive talks for charities and corporate clients about her experiences of being a young adult carer and why she thinks there could be more support for others in a similar situation.

Rochelle's book is an excellent example of sharing a personal story in a memoir style. By chronologically taking readers through her journey, she creates a compelling narrative that allows for easier storytelling. I, too, adopted this approach in my fourth book, *The Mouse That Roars*. However, when incorporating your personal story into a how-to guide format, it can be a bit more challenging. Throughout this book, I have made efforts to demonstrate how to integrate personal stories effectively, drawing from both my own experiences and those of my clients. Whilst I'm not going to talk about planning and structure in this book, I recommend you decide whether you are writing your book from a how-to perspective or memoir point of view before you start. I cover this topic in some of my other books and the Smart Author System programme.

Your perfect pitch

So, let's link back to the beginning of this chapter. Just like you would have an elevator pitch for your business, having a great pitch for your book is equally important. Imagine someone asking you to give a short précis of your book in 30 seconds or less. I'm sure you'd want to be confident and concise in your response.

This is your chance to captivate their interest and leave a lasting impression. Introduce your book with an attention-grabbing hook, clearly stating its audience and core theme. Engage your listener by highlighting the problem your book addresses and the transformative solutions it offers. Emphasise your unique angle and convey the essence of your message, showcasing its potential to captivate and inspire readers. And be sure to highlight the benefits and outcomes readers can expect. This will equip you with a strong foundation to develop an impactful and compelling pitch for your book.

Media: connecting and simplifying your message

Now that we have covered the importance of clarifying your book's vision, understanding your target audience, crafting a compelling message, and embracing your unique angle and personal story, it's time to delve into the realm of media.

In the rest of the book, I will explore the various channels and platforms through which you can effectively deliver your message to your target audience. All of this will help you to achieve the vision and goals you have in mind for your book.

THINGS TO THINK ABOUT

By getting clear on your vision for your book before you get started, you can write the right book for your business, and easily measure your success.

Consider the simple concept of market, message, and media. By being clear on your ideal reader first, you can then find out what they want to hear from you in your book, where they might be struggling, and what they want instead.

Take some time to explore your unique angle and hook. What makes your book different from other things that have already been written on your topic?

You may well be writing your book because of your own experiences and story. Get clear on this story as you write and develop your book and bring together client stories that will help to illustrate the points you want to share.

_____

_____

_____

_____

_____

_____

SECTION 1:

PRE-LAUNCH BOOK MARKETING STRATEGIES

The term 'pre-launch' refers to the period before you officially launch your book, ideally when you are still planning and writing it. In this section, I will explore pre-launch book marketing strategies that aim to simplify your marketing efforts, when you have limited time to dedicate to book marketing. My goal is to help you to leverage your book to market your business and vice versa.

It's also important to note that the strategies discussed in this section can be useful throughout the entire process of writing, publishing, and promoting your book. Therefore, select the ideas that align best with your goals and consistently apply them. Trying to do everything may lead to overwhelm and a lack of time for writing.

Whilst you may already be implementing certain marketing tactics like blogging, social media, podcasts, or videos, it's essential to adapt your messaging as you develop the content of your book. Additionally, you may consider exploring new avenues to reach your target audience effectively. Understanding your ideal reader and their preferences will be key to finding the right marketing approach. By leveraging a combination of proven methods and innovative approaches, you can effectively market your book and maximise its impact.

Although I suggest you start early with your pre-launch marketing, if you have picked up this book because you're about to publish or have already published, don't worry, it's not too late, but you may require some time to build momentum if you are not already using the techniques I mention in your marketing strategy.

CHAPTER 3
Work on your website and leverage your leads

A strong online presence is important for success and a well-designed website can make all the difference in promoting your book and connecting with your target audience. Your website serves as a window to your business, where readers can connect with your ideas, explore additional resources, and engage with your expertise. In this chapter, I will delve into the importance of a well-designed website and how it can effectively generate leads.

Leonardo da Vinci once said, "Art is never finished, it is just abandoned", and the same can be said for a website. Simply having a website is not enough. It must be carefully crafted to align with your book's focus, resonate with your audience, and ultimately drive your marketing efforts forward.

Regular updates are crucial for keeping your website relevant and found by search engines. Additionally, as you explore the ideas in your book, your understanding of your business and target audience may evolve, necessitating a website refresh. It is also possible that your book may establish you in a new niche, which could warrant a completely new website. So I recommend you review your website periodically to ensure it aligns with your message.

To maximise the effectiveness of your website, it is useful to define clear goals that align with your overall book marketing strategy.

Identify your target audience: As I have already mentioned, it's important to understand your ideal readers. Consider how your website content and design will resonate with them.

Establish your author brand: Determine the image, tone, and messaging that reflect your book's themes and your personal style as an author. Consistency across your website and your book will strengthen your brand identity.

Build your author platform: Decide how you want to position yourself as an author. Do you aim to establish expertise in a specific subject area or build a community of readers? I'm guessing it's both. Your website can serve as the central hub for your author platform, allowing you to engage with readers and fellow authors.

Showcase your book: As you approach your launch, ensure that you highlight your book prominently on your website. Create a dedicated page featuring an enticing book description, cover image, endorsements, and purchase links. This may develop as your book is created.

Establish credibility: You can utilise your website to establish your credibility as an author. Include an 'About you' page highlighting your writing experience, credentials, awards, and relevant affiliations. Testimonials or reviews from clients and readers can also enhance your credibility.

Capture leads: Your website should focus on lead generation, which I will focus on later in this chapter, and this will encourage visitors to subscribe to your email list.

Whilst it is important that your website is visually appealing, it needs to effectively market your expertise. I recommend finding a skilled web designer who can understand your requirements, make changes as required or, ideally, give you the training to make the updates yourself. Although this is another expense, if you do everything yourself, you'll never get the chance to write and publish your book!

When you start creating or updating your website, you will find there is lots of conflicting advice out there, but most importantly you want to create a site that captures the attention of your audience within seconds.

One of the things that I was taught many years ago is AIDA, and this can help you to write copy for your website, blog, videos, and other marketing. Credited to Elias St Elmo Lewis in 1898, I still believe that it's useful now, although there have been many adaptations to this strategy over the years.

AIDA stands for:

Attention
Interest
Desire
Action

Attention: To capture your audience's attention, your website and marketing materials must have an immediate impact. Within seconds, you need to make them stop and take notice. This includes engaging headlines, striking visuals, or compelling videos.

Interest: Once you have captured their attention, you need to hold your readers' interest. Shift the focus to what is interesting and valuable from their perspective rather than yours. This could include having simple messages, impactful storytelling, and thought-provoking content.

Desire: Building desire is about making your readers want what you offer. It involves evoking emotions and presenting compelling reasons why they should choose your book or engage with your expertise. This can include social proof like case studies, reviews, or testimonials and (where relevant) scarcity offers such as a time-limited special offer for your book to encourage them to take action.

Action: If AID doesn't result in any action, then nothing will happen, and all the AID will just go to waste. Ensure that every piece of marketing material you produce includes clear directions on what you want your reader to do next.

So, before I move on, why don't you take five or ten minutes to review your website right now and work out what action needs to be taken to improve the way it markets your business and your book.

It is also important that your website is found, because you could have the most beautiful website in the world, but if no one can find it, then time spent on it will be worthless. Here are some tips from Steve Bimpson to help you to do this. I will be expanding on some of the things he mentions in subsequent chapters.

 FIVE ESSENTIAL STEPS TO GET YOUR WEBSITE FOUND BY STEVE BIMPSON

You have a website. You've listened to a lot of the advice you've been given, and:

- You've spent money on a web designer and your website looks professional.

- You've made sure that your content is targeted, squarely, at your ideal client.

- Your content is all about your ideal client and his/her problems. It's focused on them, from their perspective, not on you from your perspective.

- You've considered your customer journey – the process that your typical ideal client goes through before they buy – and your website has been designed to guide them, naturally, through that journey.

- You have lead magnets, opt-in forms, and a variety of different means to engage your visitors and encourage enquiries.

- You have a well thought through follow-up process in place and ready to go.

Despite all of this, you're not happy. The problem is your website still isn't working for you, because people aren't finding it! So, what should you do?

I believe there are five essential steps that you need to take if you want the right people (your ideal clients) to find your website at the right time, i.e. when they have a problem.

Step 1: Create a web strategy

Sadly, most websites are built and, once finished, are never touched again until the next time they get overhauled – which can be years.

For your website to really work for you, think of it as a living, breathing organism that evolves and develops as you and your business grow. To achieve that requires an ongoing, ever-evolving web strategy that should be planned from the outset, informing the content you need to deliver your strategy and the schedule for it to happen.

Step 2: Do your research

There are a number of tools that can help you identify what questions your ideal clients are asking when they search online.

These include Google's Keyword Planner, Google Trends, SEO Book, Answer the Public, and Word Tracker to name a few.

You need to find out what keywords and key phrases your ideal clients are searching for online, how often these words and phrases get searched, and how competitive they are.

These results feed into your overall strategy – the idea being to create a specific blog post or piece of content that, effectively, 'answers' each individual question.

Step 3: Tell the search engines what every page is about

Every business owner I've ever spoken to loves the idea of search engines sending them more visitors. Unfortunately, that rarely happens by accident. It happens by design, but most people simply don't bother with Search Engine Optimisation (SEO). To get those all-important visitors, you need to ensure that the search engines know, precisely, what the content of any specific post or page is about. If the search engines don't know, how can they send you your ideal clients?

Step 4: Make sure everything's 'joined up'

You may be familiar with Stephen R. Covey's book, *The 7 Habits of Highly Effective People*. Habit number two is 'Always begin with the end in mind'.

Consider this with every individual piece of content on your website and ensure that you make it clear to your visitors what the next step is, how they can take it and, most importantly of all, why they should. If you don't, they almost certainly won't!

Step 5: Create a social media strategy

A lot of people post things on their social media and, although this step does include sharing your website content, there's an important step in strategy that many people tend to overlook. That is the need to actually build your social media following.

I see so many businesses continuously sharing their content to what is a fairly insignificant number of followers that are poorly targeted. Unless you have an ongoing strategy to build your social media following, the chances are your activity and content is unlikely to do you much good.

Remember...

It's important to focus your efforts in the right way and in the right direction. Too many people get hung up with numbers. They think that more visitors and more followers is what it's all about. That isn't true. What's important is that your visitors are highly targeted. You should be attracting your ideal clients because they're the ones that are going to find value in your website when they visit.

If you focus on numbers, what tends to happen is the targeting becomes far less focused and you end up in a situation that I've often come across: one where a website has a lot of visitors but they still don't get many enquiries – usually because the visitors aren't their ideal clients and, therefore, aren't interested in making an enquiry.

Steve Bimpson supports, nurtures and inspires business owners to achieve extraordinary results from their marketing and sales, making sure they thrive, rather than just survive. Find out more at www.joinedup-marketing.com.

Create a lead magnet and email opt-in

Capturing your ideal client's attention on your website isn't just about having some nice to read copy; you want people to do something, like Steve Bimpson mentioned in his piece. If you want to build a community of people who want to buy your book (and why wouldn't you?!), you need to focus on building your mailing list and have a compelling lead magnet or ethical bribe to entice your audience to join.

So, what does it mean to have a compelling lead magnet? One of my best performing lead magnets in 2009 was called 'Why you can't make money as a life coach'. Your title may be 'away from' in its message like this, or 'towards' in terms of telling people positively what they'll get from signing up. One of our lead magnets, 'The Get Started Workbook: The 21 Questions To Ask Yourself Before You Start To Write Your Book', is a good example of the latter and is particularly well received. You can download it at www.librotas.com/21questions.

If you do have a lead magnet, check that it is the right one that reflects your reader's potential journey with you. Ideally your lead magnet will lead to the next stage of working with you or encourage them to buy your book, or both. If your reader doesn't see the connection, then they won't make the leap to have a conversation with you. I'll share more on this later in this chapter.

If you are updating your lead magnet or want to put one in place, here are some things to consider:

- It should be short and actionable.
- It should solve one problem.
- It should be new, different, and compelling.

Ultimately you want your potential client and reader to come to your website and leave their contact details because they can see that you have something valuable to offer them.

I suggest you have a separate squeeze or lead page for your lead magnet, so they don't get distracted by other information on your website. Make sure the text is compelling and really dig down into what they want and tap into their emotion and logic in the copy. What problem does your lead magnet solve and why should they sign up? Make sure it is easy to register and you could consider having a sign-up box 'pop up' after someone has been on your website for a designated amount of time if your software allows you to do this.

Talking about software, there are various email marketing tools that allow you to host and deliver the lead magnet, depending upon your budget and your goal. Some will allow you to have a simple campaign, sequence and broadcast emails so you can keep in touch with subscribers, whilst others are more sophisticated and may include survey-based tools or incorporate membership functionality. Check out www.librotas.com/free for details of platforms you may wish to consider using for your email marketing.

Keep in touch with subscribers regularly

Once people sign up for your lead magnet, it's essential that you keep in touch regularly. Don't email them once and forget about them. You can create a series of autoresponders (a pre-programmed series of value-added emails) that are delivered automatically by your email marketing provider once people have registered for your lead magnet.

Then you can communicate with subscribers regularly through broadcast emails and add value through stories, tips, useful information, and the odd promotion or two! In terms of what to share, a quick tip here: multipurpose your content. You can turn your blog into a newsletter or vice versa. You could share material or updates from your book. You could also link to podcasts, videos, or any other content that you create.

Although some people believe that email marketing is dead, I disagree. But you have to give people a reason to stay in your community. You might be disheartened because in many industries newsletter 'open rates' (the number of people who open marketing emails) have dropped, and sign-ups are less common than they used to be, but it is still a model that works. It's something I've done since I started out in 2006, although my lead magnets have certainly evolved over the years. It worked for me successfully before and after I wrote and published my books.

One reason I recommend email marketing is because you own your list. Just imagine that you use one of the social media platforms to build your community and one day they shut you down (I've seen it happen!), what would you do then? That would be a huge issue if you didn't already have your own carefully curated and well-maintained list.

Let me share with you how Helen Monaghan crafted and built her list. When she started working with me on a one-to-one basis, she had a plan to write one book and went on to write two! Since we worked together, she has continued her book writing journey.

CLIENT STORY
Helen Monaghan
author of *The Magical Mix of Money & Tax*, *Successful Business Minds*, and *12 Steps to Improve Your Cashflow*

Helen employed me as her book mentor in the summer of 2015. Within ten months, she'd written not one but two books. The first one was a short e-book, *12 Steps to Improve Your Cashflow* (but it was still an impressive 10,000 words!).

The e-book served two purposes. It was the perfect download on her website where people could leave their name and email address to get a PDF copy of the book. She also uploaded it to Amazon and people could pay £1.99 if they preferred to buy it on Kindle rather than leave their contact details.

Helen's main goal for this e-book was to build her community, which she did very impressively. She shares regular content with her subscribers, has talked about her journey of writing her books, and has also promoted her products and programmes.

Both books have helped her to build a following, fill her book launch, raise her profile, attract more clients, and collaborate with other coaches and accountants.

Since launching these books, Helen has joined me on our writing retreat in Spain twice, has now completed a third book (*The Magical Mix of Money & Tax*), and is currently writing her fourth and co-authoring a fifth. Her books have already allowed her to develop products such as an online membership platform (The Financial Resilience Hub) and events which are helping her to build her business.

After creating your lead magnet, make sure that your ideal readers know it exists. Share it on your social media, in your book, the signature of your email, in podcast interviews, videos, and indeed everywhere you can!

Create your sales funnel

As well as putting your lead magnet into place, it's important to think about the next steps for your readers. Of course, once it is published, your lead magnet is likely to lead into your book. But once people have read your book, what do you want them to do next?

Most people will have a lead magnet, a book, and then a low-cost product that they sell via their website. This is normally a digital product, which means that once it has been created it needs little or none of your actual time to deliver to your clients. Next you may have something that is higher in cost, which you also may deliver one to many, such as a membership programme, workshop or event, or a higher value online product, before offering your higher ticket services. Although I'll go into more detail of specifics and examples in chapter 19, it's worth being aware of this at the pre-launch stage of your book. I suggest you note down the products and services you offer already and those which you need to develop later.

Over recent years, I have developed various funnels for Librotas with support from my team. One example of how I did this is for my ninth book, *The 7 Shifts*, which I launched as a digital book. The book includes some indispensable bonuses. Once you sign up to buy this low-cost book, you are given the chance to purchase other valuable information that complements and adds value to the book. This includes a book template which gives you everything you need to write your book using Microsoft Word and access to my signature programme, the Smart Author System. You can find out more at www.the7shifts.com.

Having a range of different products and services available means that you can leverage your time and have the right thing available for prospective clients. Some people may sign up for an online programme and others may want exclusive access to you. However, I do suggest that you find out what people want from you before you design a product that nobody wants to buy.

You don't, however, have to have all of these in place at the beginning. If you don't yet have a product, then you could create a complementary programme alongside writing your book and developing your existing content further, or you could promote your one-to-one services instead. Working with clients will give you great content for your book (and probably some great case studies). You'll also get to know what people want from you later as you work on your book. I'll go into more detail in chapter 19.

Lastly, just to remind you, if you're going to sell your books, products, and programmes, you need to nurture and develop a community of people who love what you do. You can do this through great content and regular communication. Whilst some people will simply get great value from what you share, many will want more of what you have to offer.

THINGS TO THINK ABOUT

Ensure that your website and message is clearly aimed towards your ideal client and reader. Remember that it is an ever-evolving and developing marketing tool.

Ensure your lead magnet is simple, unique, exciting, and linked closely to your book.

Make building your community and list a priority alongside writing your book. Keeping in touch with them regularly is essential, but remember you can use some of the content that ends up in your book.

Think about your reader's journey from the moment they find out about you and the next steps they might take after they've read your book.

Different levels of product will give your clients different ways they can access you and your services, and will allow you to generate multiple streams of income in your business.

_____

_____

_____

_____

_____

CHAPTER 4
Build your blog

Are you feeling overwhelmed with the idea of creating content for your marketing whilst also finding time to write your book? I completely get it. Striking the right balance is crucial. If you solely focus on marketing without dedicating time to writing, you won't have a book to promote. On the other hand, writing without marketing may result in your book bombing when you launch.

But here's the good news: in the upcoming chapters I will give you some valuable insights and shortcuts to make it easier to create content to build your community and nurture your prospective readers, starting with the power of blogging. But before I delve into this chapter further and tell you how to get started, let me share this story from Joanna Gaudoin.

CLIENT STORY
Joanna Gaudoin
author of *Getting On: Making work work*

Joanna worked with me as part of my Smart Author – Fast Track mastermind programme in 2021, as she wanted accountability to get her book written. In the first few weeks of the Smart Author programme, we spend time discussing who their books are for and the key messages. Despite being an organised person, Joanna recognised that she never planned her university essays, she just wrote them. It quickly became clear this was not possible for a book!

To create a structure that worked for her book, Joanna decided to develop a spreadsheet. She never intended it to become so large but by the time she had gone through all her client notes and slides and put one topic/piece of guidance on each row of a spreadsheet she had several hundred rows. However, it was then fairly easy to put overarching topics and a subtopic against each which led to the chapter development!

When she showed her fellow authors and myself the spreadsheet (apparently my face was a picture!), they were a bit daunted but it was the method that worked for Joanna. It made sure that she knew what she was writing about each time she sat down to write and she worked systematically through the chapter topics.

Now, you might be wondering why this client story is in a chapter about creating content for blogs. Well, just imagine you created a spreadsheet like this as part of your book planning. Not only would it help you to write your book, but it would also give you hundreds of topics for blogs and articles, videos and podcasts, social media posts, email marketing, and so much more! But before we get carried away, let's get stuck into the business case for blogging!

Why blog?

Whether you blog already or want to start one alongside your book, blogging can be a great way to find your voice and start sharing your message. And if you're a natural writer like me (I've had a blog since I started out in business in 2006), you'll probably find blogging easy. If you don't blog already or you're sporadic in your approach, you might wonder why it's important.

Blogging is a great way to grow a community of people who want to read your book; it's free and only requires your time once your blog is set up. In effect you're writing short articles which you publish on your website. These can be used to help your readers and showcase how you can support them.

There are many reasons why I love blogging. When you talk about things that are relevant to your book, it enables people to engage with you, especially when you invite them to comment on your writing, share your posts, and they could potentially become your client.

It's relatively easy to add a blog to your website, especially if you have a WordPress site, and if you enjoy writing – which I hope you do! – this is a perfect way to share your message with more people.

Here are some advantages of blogging:

- Internet search engines love new content and having regular blogs and updates will help drive traffic to your website, thus enabling your prospective clients and readers to find you online.

- When you have an effective strategy, you can connect with your audience by providing regular compelling content.

- When your readers connect with your blog posts, they will become interested in what you have to say. It gives you the chance to stand out and build your credibility and authority before you've actually been published.

- You can generate more leads and subscribers to your mailing list, or you can promote your services by writing relevant articles that relate to your next promotion.

If you choose to blog, it's important to be consistent in terms of how often you post a new article, but remember all of the strategies in this book are designed to be easy to implement around writing your book. Let me share some of these now.

Develop and repurpose your content

As I mentioned earlier, blogging about topics related to your book provides a valuable opportunity to repurpose and develop your content. When your message is aligned, blogging becomes easier and helps you to create high-quality material. You can leverage relevant sections from your book, expanding on them for engaging blog posts.

Furthermore, blogging offers multiple benefits. It allows you to get feedback from readers, address their questions, generate interest in your upcoming book, and explore specific subjects in greater detail. Your blog can also serve as a platform to react to topical and newsworthy items, enabling you to share your unique perspective through insightful blog posts.

This is how Sheryl Andrews used blogging and videos to support writing her first book. Through this process, she realised the symbiotic relationship between marketing and book writing, as each supports and enhances the other.

CLIENT STORY
Sheryl Andrews
author of *Manage your Critic – From Overwhelm to Clarity in 7 Steps*

My client, friend, and now colleague, Sheryl Andrews, first attended my writing retreat in Spain in 2015. She then published her first book in the autumn of 2016. She used her blog, networking, and video to build her followers by charting her writing journey.

Although it might feel like a distraction, Sheryl says, "It helped me to develop some of the concepts in my book and it meant I was much more effective when it came to blogging and communicating online. I really had to think about who I was writing the blog to. This resulted in some great feedback and helped me to develop my own style of writing."

By producing impromptu videos, where she talked from the heart, she was able to transcribe her own words for written content. She goes on to say, "Once I realised that marketing and book writing were one and the same, I understood how they mutually supported each other. The blogging and video posts gave me in-the-moment feedback that what I was saying resonated and committing to writing a book really focused my mind on what was important and my core message." This helped her to bring the book together as well as helping to build interest in her book. This led to her successfully pre-selling her book prior to its official launch.

Conversely, you can also use your blog to aid in creating content for your book. By repurposing blog posts, articles, or other long form written pieces you have already produced, you can integrate them into the relevant chapters of your book. This approach saves time and prevents duplication, allowing you to focus on filling any gaps and refining the material you've already created.

Create your blog ideas

If you find yourself struggling to come up with ideas for your blog, let me give you some guidance:

- Draw inspiration from conversations with clients and prospects. Often, these interactions involve answering their questions and addressing their concerns, which can be transformed into informative blog posts. By doing so, you not only provide relevant content to your audience but also nurture and strengthen the relationship with your prospective clients.

- Use the information gathered from surveys, questionnaires, or interviews. This valuable data can serve as a foundation for your blog posts. Consider addressing the most common questions or difficulties that your audience is facing, providing practical solutions and insights, which also helps establish credibility within your niche.

- Employ the strategy of case studies. When one of your clients gets amazing outcomes as a result of working with you, take the opportunity to interview them. This interview can be transformed into recorded content and serve as the basis for a blog post.

By implementing these approaches, you can generate a steady stream of engaging and relevant blog ideas while avoiding repetition and leveraging different sources of inspiration. In terms of the different type of blog posts styles you could use, follow Ginny Carter's advice.

 ## SIX IDEAS FOR BLOG POSTS TO PROMOTE YOUR BOOK BY GINNY CARTER

Blogging is an obvious way to promote your book, because when you use your blog to discuss and explain the topics in it you give your audience a taste of what they'll experience if they go on to buy the book itself.

However, if you're like many people, you might sometimes struggle to come up with ideas for your blog. Don't worry, we all get stuck. It helps when you realise that there are different types of blog posts for promoting your book. Once you've got your head around them, exciting ideas will flow as you see how you can tackle your topic in new ways.

There are many options, but here are six of them to get you started.

1. The series of excerpts

This is so obvious and yet rarely used. You've written your book, so why not lift some of the material from it and create a series of blog posts? You'll need to tweak it so that it's 'blog friendly' and also makes sense outside of the context of your book, but it's an easy win.

2. The how to

This does what it says on the tin. You tell your readers how to do something they find hard and you find easy, on a subject related to your book.

3. The interview

This is where you interview various experts on a topic related to your book. The great thing about this is it gives you an excellent excuse to contact influencers in your niche; if they like what they read they'll also share it on social media, and by doing so spread the news about your book.

4. The case study

This post tells a story which 'proves' the points that you make in your book. Giving an example of someone else who succeeded by following your methods lends your expertise extra credibility. You can link the case study to your book in a couple of ways: by repurposing a story you already tell in your book, or by writing a new story related to it.

5. The list post

What resources would your readers need to get the most out of your book? How about creating a long list post which gives them links to everything they need? You can refer back to your book within the post so that your blog readers know where to go to find out more on the subject.

6. The why post

As the name suggests, this post examines the causes of one of the issues you've written about in your book. It's more reflective, and sometimes more challenging, than some of the other options. In this you delve into the problems troubling your readers, offering your wisdom on the causes and suggesting solutions.

In fact, once you hit on a great topic which relates to your book and resonates with your readers, you can write about it again and again using the formulae above. This is a brilliant way to become known for your expertise and for your book to shine.

Remember always to mention your book in each post and to provide a link to where people can buy it. If it's yet to be published, add an email sign-up link for those who want to be notified when it's hit the virtual shelves.

Ginny Carter is a business book ghostwriter, book coach, and award-winning author. You can find out more about her work at www.marketingtwentyone.co.uk.

To generate ideas, one of the things that I do is to record every idea as it pops into my head – sometimes on the back of an envelope, a sticky note, or anything else I have to hand! Sometimes this is when I'm speaking with a client or friend; at other times it may be something I've read that inspires me.

There are various note apps you can use when all you have to hand is your smartphone, or you can dictate your ideas directly into your device. This means that you can record your ideas rather than lose them! This helps you to ensure you have a constant source of ideas to refer to when you are writing a new blog post.

You could also add these ideas to an online project management tool to keep all of your ideas in one place or add them to a Word document if it makes it easier for you. I do the latter as it allows me to create the relevant blog when I'm ready and I often will write multiple blogs in one day when I feel inspired. I was recently advised to have an annual plan for all of my blog posts, which admittedly I don't do, but I've always got ideas that are linked to my upcoming events, promotions, and themes that I want to talk about.

How to write your blog posts

Whilst this is not a book specifically about blogging, I'd like to share a few tips on writing your blog posts.

Break down your topic: For blogging (or actually any form of longer content), break down your topic ideas into small chunks. For example, I could easily write an article about marketing a book, but where would I start and where would I finish? I could easily write an article about using blogging to market a book, but again this is a big topic. So, I could break this down into sub-articles. Here are five examples:

- 5 Effective Strategies to Promote Your Book Through Blogging
- The Power of Blogging: How to Build a Strong Author Platform
- Using SEO Techniques to Boost Book Visibility Through Blogging
- Engaging Your Readers: How to Craft Compelling Blog Content for Book Promotion
- From Blog to Book: Repurposing Blog Content for Successful Book Creation

Start with a compelling introduction: Grab readers' attention from the beginning with a strong SEO-friendly headline and captivating introduction. Use an intriguing hook, ask thought-provoking questions, or share a relatable story to draw readers in and make them want to continue reading.

Provide valuable and well-structured content: Offer valuable insights, practical advice, or entertaining stories that are relevant to your audience. Organise your content into logical sections with headings and subheadings, making it easy to skim and digest and use bullet points or numbered lists to enhance readability.

Include visuals: Incorporate eye-catching visuals, such as images, infographics, or videos, to enhance your blog post. Visuals can help break up the text, illustrate concepts, and make your content more engaging and shareable. Ensure the visuals are high quality, relevant, and properly credited.

Encourage interaction and provide a clear call to action: Engage readers by including opportunities for interaction. Encourage comments, ask questions, or conduct polls to encourage readers to share their thoughts and experiences. Or end your blog post with a clear call to action, guiding readers to take the desired next step, whether it's subscribing to your newsletter, sharing the post on social media, or exploring related content.

Proofread and edit your blog post: Before publishing your blog post, take the time to proofread and edit it carefully. Check for grammatical errors, spelling mistakes, and awkward sentence structures. Ensure that your ideas flow smoothly and coherently. Consider reading the post aloud or asking someone else to review it for a fresh perspective. Pay attention to formatting, consistency in style, and proper use of punctuation. A well-edited and error-free blog post enhances your credibility and professionalism.

Use AI to help refine your content: Consider using a tool like ChatGPT to refine and enhance your blog post content. You can use it to generate ideas (it came up with the list of ideas above); it can help improve the clarity and flow of your writing and it can provide valuable insights and suggestions that can improve the quality of your blog posts. Just remember to review and tailor your post to align with your writing style so that the resulting blog sounds like you.

Optimise your blog post for SEO: To maximise the visibility and reach of your blog post and help it to be found, consider your SEO as Steve Bimpson mentioned in the previous chapter. Conduct keyword research, such as using the Google Keyword Planner to identify keywords related to your topic, and strategically place them in your blog post's title, headings, subheadings, and throughout the content. You may also choose to use a free SEO tool like All-in-One SEO and Yoast, both of which are WordPress plugins. I particularly like Yoast's traffic light system that allows you to see at a glance whether your blog post is optimised and makes suggestions to help you to get more organic traffic to your website.

Promote and share your blog post across multiple channels:
After publishing your blog post, it's crucial to actively promote and share it across various channels to increase its visibility and reach. Share your blog post on your social media platforms, such as Facebook, Twitter, LinkedIn, and Instagram, with compelling captions and relevant hashtags. You can share your latest content with your newsletter subscribers and encourage readers to share your blog post by including social sharing buttons on your blog, making it effortless for them to spread the word.

Lastly, after you've written a blog post, don't just share it once, share it multiple times! You could create an editorial calendar, which although it sounds grand, simply entails creating an Excel spreadsheet with four columns.

In the first column detail the date on which your blog post is published. In the second column, insert the title. In the fourth column, insert the web address of the specific blog post, then copy the row five times. Then fill in column three with five updates you could share on social media so you can repurpose the blog post five different times with five different messages. There will be more on social media posts in chapter 8.

You can download a sample editorial calendar at www.librotas.com/free so that you can easily get started.

Become a guest blogger

If starting your own blog at this stage is a step too far or you want to reach a new market, another option is to be a guest blogger for complementary businesses that share your target readership. You also might craft articles that you share on digital publishing sites or online magazines or even longer LinkedIn articles.

I used to use Ezinearticles.com to share my longer form posts and, most recently, online article sites such as Medium and Substack now offer you opportunities to share your expertise, personal stories, and thought-provoking content with a global audience.

Medium is an influential online article site. It is a diverse publishing platform, attracting a wide range of voices and perspectives. Medium offers a seamless reading experience and encourages engagement through its 'clap' feature, which allows readers to show appreciation for articles. The platform is known for its curated collections and publications, making it easy for readers to discover high-quality content on various topics, from technology and business to personal development and lifestyle. Medium also provides you with the opportunity to monetise your work through the Medium Partner Program, which allows for earnings based on member reading time.

Substack is a rapidly growing platform that enables you to build your own newsletters and distribute them directly to your subscribers. It has gained traction as a preferred platform for independent writers, journalists, and thought leaders seeking more autonomy and control over their content and monetisation. Substack offers a straightforward interface, allowing you to focus on crafting engaging content while the platform handles the technical aspects of newsletter distribution. Substack operates on a subscription model, enabling writers to generate income by offering exclusive content to their subscribers.

If you select one of these routes, it will take time to build your audience and you will need a strong biography, professional photograph, and link to your website or book.

 **THINGS TO THINK ABOUT**

If blogging isn't part of your marketing strategy, then I'd advise you to think about including it.

Don't reinvent the wheel by continually creating new content; just find ways to repurpose what you know already. Share snippets from your book to get feedback from your readers. And remember to consider what you have already written which may go into your book.

Less is more. Choose to take a helicopter overview on a subject or go deeper into a smaller topic.

Keep a record of all of your ideas, even if you don't write about these topics now. Find a system that works for you that enables you to keep all of your ideas in one place.

You don't have to rely solely on your own blog. Look for other opportunities to guest blog or write articles for other publications.

_____

_____

_____

_____

_____

CHAPTER 5
Publicise with podcasts

If blogging isn't really your thing or you want to find another way of creating content for your book and marketing it at the same time, I want to show you an alternative method of sharing your message. Consider marketing your book through podcasts.

A podcast is an audio-based form of digital media that allows you to create and distribute content to a global audience. Podcasts are typically available for streaming or downloading, and listeners can access them on various platforms and devices.

We've seen podcasts become increasingly popular over recent years as many people want to consume information in bitesize chunks and increasing numbers tune into podcasts during their commutes, workouts, or leisure time. More people using smartphones and the wider variety of platforms available have contributed to their popularity.

For the content creator, podcasts have become a favoured way of sharing short snippets of information with their audience, because they create an intimate and immersive experience. It allows you to share personal stories, opinions, and expertise with your audience.

My first book, *The Secrets of Successful Coaches*, was born out of 11 interviews with successful coaches. When I launched the book, I also carried out over 20 interviews with other experts that helped to support the book's launch and contributed to its success.

Myself or one of my team often carry out interviews with clients when they've launched their books to chat about their challenges and successes, and also to help their book to reach more people.

Although they are not officially podcasts in the true sense of the word – as they are recorded as videos and also turned into audio files – they are still great content which can be used to build awareness of what we do and promote our authors. Check out our latest interviews and content at our download link: www.librotas.com/free.

As part of the launch for the second edition of *Book Marketing Made Simple*, I am starting my own podcast. You can search for 'Business Book Bites' wherever you find your podcasts.

I love podcasts because they give you an easy way to share your information and you can also collaborate with other experts and share your knowledge with both of your communities.

Now, before you jump in with both feet and say "Yes, I'm going to start recording podcasts", find out whether your clients will actually listen to them. If they are busy people and like to listen to great information on the go, then it's certainly something to consider. And before you get started, consider these tips by podcast expert Steve Randall.

 FIVE WAYS PODCASTING CAN SUPPORT YOUR BOOK LAUNCH BY STEVE RANDALL

Having a podcast is a powerful tool for building authority and defining your expertise. Here are some of my top tips for how podcasting can support your book and its launch.

1. Presence

The more that people see (or hear) your name and are exposed to your content, the more you become established in their minds as the expert on your topic.

Being on podcast platforms such as Apple Podcasts, Spotify, and Google Podcasts also helps you to be found in search engines, plus they are search engines in their own right – when someone looks for you in a podcast app, you need to be there!

2. Authenticity

There is nothing more powerful than hearing something directly from the source, especially in today's cynical world. A podcast gives you the chance to talk directly to your audience and build rapport and a feeling that your potential readers 'know' you, which in turn increases the chance of them buying your book.

3. Anticipation

Creating a buzz and building anticipation is a tried and tested strategy for any launch and a podcast is a great way to do this for your book.

It doesn't have to be an ongoing endeavour; a short series of just three or four episodes, focusing on key pillars of your book (and perhaps an excerpt), is a great way to generate interest.

Schedule them in the immediate run-up to your book release. They don't have to be lengthy – 5 or 10 minutes used well will get your ideas into ears!

4. Versatility

Once you have the audio recorded, you can repurpose it in multiple ways.

Use 'audiogram' videos to share full episodes on video platforms and shorter clips on social media.

Use the audio as a soundtrack to a slideshow or use a transcript as the basis for a written article.

5. Reach

My final tip is to get booked on other people's podcasts. Seek out shows that already engage your target audience and with a strong social media presence. This is a great opportunity to be heard and benefit from someone else's marketing efforts, while also adding to your presence and authenticity.

Steve Randall is the founder of Communication Generation, a podcast production company based in Hampshire, UK. With a background in radio, Steve brings affordable audio production and consultancy to coaches, consultants and entrepreneurs. Find out more at CGpods.com.

You can also listen to an interview I carried out with Steve Randall on the topic of podcasts on my download page: www.librotas.com/free. Steve also works with me and some of my clients to help us with our podcasts!

Where to start with podcasts

When thinking about doing your own podcast, the first thing you might be asking is "Where do I start?", so here are some additional tips to help you.

Select a captivating theme and topics: Choose a catchy name for your podcast that links in with your theme and will help attract and retain your ideal listeners. This could be the same as the title for your book or linked in with your business name or niche. Then think about what topics your audience would like to listen to – you can follow some of the strategies in the blogging chapter for this. This could be the top 20 questions people ask you or the top 20 questions that your prospects and clients should be asking you but don't!

Develop a strong structure: Plan the format and structure of your podcast episodes. Consider whether you'll have interviews, monologues, segments, or a combination of different elements and how long each episode is likely to be. Having a consistent structure helps maintain audience engagement.

Research and prepare: Plan your podcasts in advance so you know what you are likely to cover, when they will be recorded and the expected day of release. For each podcast, thoroughly research your topic to provide accurate and valuable information to your listeners. Prepare an outline or script to ensure the smooth flow of content, depending upon how much information you need to deliver it seamlessly.

Be authentic and genuine: Your listeners want to connect with you, so be yourself. Share your unique perspective, thoughts, and experiences. Authenticity builds trust and creates a deeper connection with your audience. Use personal anecdotes, case studies, or examples to illustrate your points and captivate your listeners.

Consistency is key: If you decide to create podcasts as part of your book and business marketing strategy, like blogging, I suggest you do them regularly, as people will come to expect them. To keep it simple, you could choose to host standalone series rather than weekly podcasts, as this gives you a breather every now and then and time to create your next series!

Develop an easy-to-follow process: Having a structured process in place will make it easier for you to consistently produce podcasts for your audience. By implementing standard elements such as intro music, a standard introduction, the main body, and outro music, you can save time and maintain a consistent approach.

I will move on to the technology in a moment, in respect to what you need to set up and record your podcast, but I thought it pertinent to mention AI here. In the last chapter I noted how it can be used for blogging and many people also find it effective for supporting a podcast, as it can free up your time and stimulate your creativity. For example, I recently used ChatGPT to come up with a shortlist of titles for my own podcast. You can use specific AI tools that can help you to produce show notes, transcripts, and summaries for each episode, and you can also use AI to help refine your topics, do some research, and give you new ideas that you haven't thought about yourself.

What tech and equipment do you need?

To create your own podcast, you will need a good quality microphone, editing software to produce and edit your recording, artwork and copy to help promote your podcast, and a podcast platform that enables you to easily distribute your podcast.

You could choose to use a recording studio to record your podcasts and/or outsource the editing to a podcast expert to help edit and put together your podcasts. Although this will impact on your budget, it will give you time to write! When you work with an expert, they will make sure you don't make any mistakes with the production of your podcast and they should also be able to advise on any legal considerations, such as permissions, copyright, and music licences, so you don't make any expensive errors.

When your podcast is available to stream on platforms, such as Apple Podcasts and Spotify, you will reach a wider audience. People who know you can subscribe to your podcast and those who don't know you can find your podcast via the search function if they are interested in your topic. As with blogging, you need to optimise your metadata so people can find you. It is also good practice to tell your community about each new podcast that you record. You can do this through social media, your blog, and your newsletter.

If you want to start your own podcast, begin by subscribing to other podcasts. See what you like and can relate to, and what you think your prospective listeners will enjoy. Podcasts will help you to reach a worldwide audience, so take this into account with your message.

There are ways you can monetise your podcast if you wish. This includes sponsorship, crowdfunding, and premium subscriptions, but when you start out, you will likely fund the process yourself.

And as with any form of marketing, check your metrics. Regularly view your download numbers, listener feedback and reviews, and subscriber growth.

Take a moment now to hear from Alison Colley who is using podcasts to promote her business.

HOW PODCASTING HAS HELPED MY BUSINESS
BY ALISON COLLEY

Podcasting in the UK has increased in popularity over the last few years and there are large range of podcasts on all kinds of topics available, but the volume of UK podcasters is still less than content creators on other platforms. As a result you may still find that you are one of only a couple of people in the same area of expertise.

I have been podcasting as a method of promoting my business for almost nine years and I have made many new connections and extended my reach to a wider and different audience during this time. It has increased my credibility as an expert in my field and has given me something different or unique to talk about with clients, contacts, and potential clients.

Here's my advice if you want to build podcasting into your business:

1. Be consistent

Like many other forms of marketing you have to maintain consistency and show up on a regular basis. In the early stages, when your downloads are low and you are not receiving any feedback from listeners, it can be disheartening, but as long as you are enjoying doing it keep going, for a minimum of six months to a year, in order to get a real idea if it is going to work for your business.

2. Use podcasting to improve your confidence

Aside from the benefits to the business I have also found that podcasting has helped me to develop my public speaking skills, as whilst you can easily edit your podcast if you make a mistake, you will find that mistakes become fewer as you grow in confidence and perfect your style. This in turn gives you the confidence and experience when standing up and speaking in public.

3. You can do it on a budget

The good thing about podcasting is it is inexpensive and easy to get started. You only need a computer, microphone, and internet connection. Whilst good quality sound for your podcast is crucial, you don't need to spend lots of money and can purchase a suitable microphone for around £30.

4. Put your podcast on YouTube

There is software available to convert the audio to a video for YouTube; I use Headliner. It's a great way to reach a new audience and you will be surprised how many people listen to podcasts on YouTube without any visuals.

If you have something to say and are thinking about it, listen to some other podcasts to see what works and what doesn't, and then just give it a go!

Alison Colley is an employment law solicitor specialising in all aspects of employment law and HR. Alison's podcast is The Employment Law & HR Podcast which can be found on iTunes, Stitcher and online at www.realemploymentlawadvice.co.uk/podcast.

Become a podcast guest

If you don't want to have your own podcast, I strongly advise that you guest on other people's podcasts, as Steve Randall alluded to earlier. Over the years, I've done many telesummits, online conferences, and interviews. These have given me great content for my community, helped me to reach more people in other people's communities, and built my credibility. I'll touch more on this later, as this is a great launch and post-launch strategy.

 **THINGS TO THINK ABOUT**

If you enjoy talking, then podcasts may be a good addition to your marketing, but remember you don't have to do everything I suggest.

Think about the top 20 questions your clients are asking you, and the 20 questions that they should be asking you. Then answer these in your podcasts.

There are plenty of things to consider, so you may choose to work with an expert who can help you to produce a high-quality product.

Your podcast can be published on all of the popular streaming services, allowing people to find you easily, which will help to build your community.

You also may wish to interview other people or be interviewed, both of which will allow you to collaborate with other experts and serve both of your communities.

_____

_____

_____

_____

_____

CHAPTER 6
Go viral with video

Video is a powerful tool for book marketing. With its ability to captivate and engage audiences visually, it enables you to effectively promote your business and book.

By incorporating video into various aspects of your promotional efforts, you can create a more immersive and impactful experience for your audience, enhance your online presence, build a personal connection with potential readers, and ultimately boost book sales and business engagement.

In essence, creating videos can be relatively simple. You can just take your smartphone, set up your lighting, record a piece to camera, and then upload it to YouTube or TikTok in minutes, or you can go live into one of the social media platforms, like LinkedIn, Facebook, or Instagram and deliver valuable content.

In reality, you don't need to be the person in front of the camera to create great videos. There are platforms where you can record videos without needing to be in front of the screen, such as using presentation sharing platforms or other screen recording software, animated videos, whiteboard videos, and videos overlaid with images and a voice-over. The list is always growing and expanding!

In this chapter, I will explore the role of video in book marketing, highlighting its benefits, and show you how it can be effectively incorporated into a comprehensive marketing strategy.

How to use video

There are dozens of ways you can use videos in your book marketing campaign, and I have included my favourite innovative approaches here. You can select the strategies that best align with your book, target audience, and marketing goals.

An introduction to you on your website: Create a compelling video that introduces you to visitors, allowing them to quickly get to know you and understand how you can help them. This video creates a powerful way to make a personal connection with potential readers.

Book introduction video on your book's sales page: Develop a book-specific video that highlights the key aspects and benefits of your book. This video should align with the information provided earlier in terms of effectively pitching your book, and should entice potential readers to order your book.

Video on your lead magnet page: Craft a compelling video to communicate the value and benefits of your lead magnet, motivating your reader to take action and sign up. As a result, this will help build your mailing list.

Vlogs (video blogs): Consider creating video content in the form of vlogs, similar to written blogs or podcasts. Share informative snippets on specific topics related to your book, either through live videos on social media platforms or pre-recorded content shared across various channels.

Marketing for events and workshops: Capture and share video snippets of yourself delivering content during events or workshops. These videos can be used to market future events, as they will showcase your expertise and engage with potential attendees. Additionally, you could compile a showreel highlighting your speaking engagements to promote yourself as a speaker.

Event recordings: Consider recording and packaging your events for future sales. By offering these recorded events to those who attended and to new audiences, you can generate additional revenue and extend the reach of your expertise.

Client testimonials: Capture short video testimonials from clients who have attended your events or worked with you. These testimonials can serve as powerful social proof, demonstrating the value and impact of your services. Consider recording both brief testimonials immediately after events and more comprehensive video interviews, as discussed in the previous chapter.

Longer video content: Develop longer video material that you can offer as part of a freebie or a paid video series. This in-depth content can provide valuable insights, further establish your authority in your niche, and serve as an additional revenue stream.

Book readings: Record yourself reading excerpts from your book or sharing significant pieces either whilst you are writing it or when published. This allows potential readers to experience your writing style first hand, creating intrigue and encouraging them to delve deeper into your book.

Author interviews: Conduct interviews with other authors (or experts or collaborators of your book) to generate interest and engage with potential readers. These interviews can provide valuable insights, discussions about writing processes, or even collaborative book promotions.

Collaborate with influencers or other entrepreneurs: Partner with other relevant content creators to create collaborative videos. This could include joint discussions, book-related challenges, or even hosting live Q&A sessions, tapping into the influencer's audience and expanding your reach.

Book-themed discussions or panels: Host video discussions or panels centred around book-related topics. Invite other authors, experts, or enthusiasts in your genre to join the conversation and provide diverse perspectives. This not only offers valuable insights but also expands your network and introduces your book to new audiences.

Behind-the-scenes author journey: Document your writing process, research adventures, or the inspirations behind your book through behind-the-scenes videos, which offer an intimate look into your author's journey.

Animated videos: Consider creating or outsourcing animated videos that visually depict key concepts or themes from your book. Using a tool such as VideoScribe, animation can add a visually captivating element and make complex ideas more accessible and engaging for viewers.

Book-related tutorials or how-to videos: Share instructional videos related to topics explored in your book. This positions you as an authority while providing valuable content to your audience.

Book giveaways and unboxings: Record videos where you announce and showcase book giveaways or unboxings of your own book. This generates excitement and buzz, encouraging viewers to participate and share the video.

Book trailers: One of the tried-and-true methods of promoting a book is through the creation of book trailers. Book trailers are short videos that provide a visual representation of your book's essence, capturing the attention of potential readers and enticing them to explore further. They function similarly to movie trailers, offering a sneak peek into the themes in your book.

Link to other people's video recordings of you: Instead of always producing your own recordings, consider incorporating other people's video recordings of you, such as TEDx Talks or conference presentations. These can significantly enhance your book marketing efforts and reinforce your credibility. Remember to obtain permission and attribute the videos appropriately to ensure compliance with copyright and usage restrictions.

Wow, that is quite a list, isn't it! Although video isn't my primary platform of choice, I have embraced its power in my book marketing efforts. For instance, my book launch for *The Mouse That Roars* was recorded, allowing me to use the talk as a promotional tool. It was featured on the speaker page of my website, showcasing my speaking abilities to potential event organisers. Additionally, I have recorded videos of other events, complete with testimonials that demonstrate the positive impact of attending those events. I often direct people to my TEDx Talk, which hugely boosts my credibility.

In 2016, I shared my top ten tips for writing a book through a video that not only created engaging blog posts but also became a lead magnet on my website, attracting aspiring authors. Furthermore, I promote the 'Get Started' workbook mentioned in chapter 3 with a video displayed on my website.

My signature programme, the Smart Author System, delivers its content through a series of short videos, providing aspiring authors with a comprehensive six-week programme from idea to publishing and marketing their book.

During our recent writing retreat in Spain, I recorded some blog-style videos and we captured testimonials from our clients, showcasing their experiences and the value they derived from the retreat.

A shining example of someone who embraces video in his business is Steve Judge, who effectively promoted his first book, *Don't Lean On Your Excuses*, by regularly recording video blogs to chart his author's journey and celebrate his success. I took a similar approach with my pre-launch marketing for the second edition of this book.

Six steps to create compelling videos

Often when a business owner creates a video for the first time they spend too long playing with the shiny stuff: the camera and the editing software. Conversely, they spend little time on the two most critical elements of the video: the script and what they actually want to achieve.

Here are six steps to creating compelling videos that I originally learnt from my good friend and colleague, Mark Edmunds. The most important stage of creating any piece of marketing is the planning, and it's exactly the same with video.

Before starting on your next video, follow these six steps, and you will create a compelling video that actually has the chance of being watched all the way to the end and potentially going viral.

1. Why are you creating the video?

The most important thing you need to know is why you are investing time, money, and energy in creating videos.

What is its purpose and how is it going to help you and your business?

What do you want your audience to do when they watch the video?

What does a successful video project look like?

Knowing the answer to these questions will help you formulate the right message.

2. Who are you targeting?

A common mistake in all marketing is being too general. Being general does not work as you cannot specifically appeal to everyone.

So you need to know your target audience. Who are they, what do they look like, what are their problems, what do they do, where do they shop, what are their goals in life, what are their trigger points and what do they want? (If you've already read and actioned the information in chapter 2, this will be familiar to you.) The more you can narrow it down to your perfect or ideal client avatar, the better!

The clearer you are at understanding who you want to work with, the easier it will be for you to formulate a script to talk about their problems and desires using their words, terminology, and language patterns. This means they are more likely to be engaged by your videos because they feel you understand them and what they want in life.

A great way to get results is to create a 'client avatar' of who you want to work with and then give this a real name and persona, such as 'Sarah', a single mum in her thirties, who lives locally and has a specific interest in your area of expertise. Then it allows you to create a mental picture of them in your mind.

3. It is all about them

Now you know what you and your ideal clients desire, it's time to start formulating your message either in the form of a 'word for word' script to use on a teleprompter, or a series of carefully planned bullet points to keep you on track when ad-libbing to camera. However, before you get carried away thinking about what you can tell your viewers, remember one thing: your viewers will not care about you and your message when watching the video. Instead, when they first watch your video, all they will be thinking about is themselves and how they are going to benefit.

When crafting your message, ensure that they will gain something, whether that's an understanding of how you could help them, or even something actionable that they can use to achieve something in their business or personal life straight away.

4. Use spoken language and do not try to be perfect

If you are writing a script to use on a teleprompter remember that you are creating something to be spoken aloud. Therefore throw the grammar book out the window and write 'spoken English'. Use abbreviations, put pauses in as though you are thinking (um, err), start sentences with 'and', keep your language simple, and make sure your script is easy to read out loud.

This last point is critical as it will prevent you from wasting time and money tripping over your own tongue and feeling highly frustrated because your videos do not sound natural. Being conversational, umming, erring and occasionally making the odd mistake in your videos is a good thing as it will make you more believable and authentic to the viewer and more approachable as a person.

5. Speak to one person

Your videos will be watched by many people – hundreds, thousands, tens of thousands – and, with luck, many more.

However even though many people will watch them, you will get a better level of engagement if you create your videos as though they are just for 'one' important viewer. This is because everyone who fits with your 'client avatar' will have a sense that it's a personal message for them and that they are special rather than just part of a larger online audience.

Speak to this one person (remember 'Sarah' who I mentioned earlier?). By doing this, you will find it an easier experience for you than trying to engage with a cold piece of plastic and glass also known as a video camera. In addition, your videos will be far warmer and easier to watch for your audience.

6. Write your script

There are many different ways to script your videos. One of the simplest is the Hook, Path, and Persuasion technique, which consists of three parts:

Part 1. The hook: Grab their attention

You only have a few seconds to gain the attention of your target audience, so make sure your script starts with a bang! Grab them by demonstrating you understand the exact problem they want to be rid of or give them a fact which makes them sit up and think 'I need to know more!'

Part 2. The path: Take them on a journey

Now you have got their interest, you need to keep them engaged by taking them on a logical journey towards the most important element of your script – the call to action. On this journey give them enough information so that when they get to the end of the video they feel they can trust you and want to follow your call to action. To do this, your video needs to address their 'perceived' problem and show that you can help them solve it.

This may be through education on what they need to do (but not how to do it); by demonstrating how you have helped others through success stories of other clients; or by actually solving their problem in the video but then introducing a bigger and far more scary problem.

Part 3. The persuasion: Tell them what to do

Finally, you need to get them to take action by telling them to specifically do something. Failing to do this means that they are likely to watch the video but then move onto something else, such as the next video of a cute kitten or a kid falling off a skateboard on YouTube or Facebook.

Tell them to 'pick up the phone and give me a call to discover xyz' or 'share this video with your friends because y' or 'sign up for the event today and you will get abc extra'.

Remember to use scarcity to get the best results by giving them a reason to do it NOW. Otherwise, they are likely to procrastinate until they forget about you.

Hosting and distributing your video

With video, you also need to think about how you host and distribute it.

YouTube offers a free option for video hosting and distribution. However, there are additional features and benefits available through YouTube Premium, a subscription-based service that removes ads, provides offline viewing, and offers access to exclusive content.

To distribute your videos on YouTube, create a YouTube channel and upload your videos following their guidelines. You can optimise your video titles, descriptions, tags, and thumbnail images to improve discoverability. You can engage with viewers through comments, likes, and shares. You can also leverage YouTube's features like end screens and cards to direct viewers to your book's website or other related videos.

Vimeo offers both free and paid plans. The free plan has limitations on video storage and bandwidth, while paid plans provide increased storage, advanced analytics, and customisation options.

To distribute videos on Vimeo, create an account and upload your videos to your profile. You can customise the video player, privacy settings, and video appearance to align with your branding. Vimeo offers various tools and integrations for embedding videos on your website or sharing them on social media platforms. It also provides analytics to track video performance and engagement.

Additionally, beyond YouTube and Vimeo, you can share your videos directly onto your preferred social media site, or simply go live directly into one of these sites or by using a platform like Streamyard (which enables you to go live into multiple platforms at the same time).

Lastly, TikTok has quickly risen in popularity and is currently a free platform for video sharing and distribution. It offers various creative tools and features, such as filters, effects, music, and text overlays, to enhance your videos. TikTok enables you to reach a wide audience beyond your existing followers, as the platform recommends content based on users' interests and engagement patterns.

TikTok is known for its viral challenges and trends, so participate in popular challenges that align with your book's theme or create book-themed challenges that engage viewers and encourage them to interact with your content.

Since TikTok is primarily used for short and engaging videos, you need to capture your viewer's attention quickly and provide entertaining or informative content in a concise format. Experiment with different storytelling techniques, behind-the-scenes peeks, book recommendations, or engaging snippets related to your book.

When you use relevant and popular hashtags in your video captions you will increase discoverability and reach. Research trending hashtags in the book community or create your own book-related hashtags (check out #booktok) to build a community around your content.

You can multipurpose any videos you create on TikTok onto Instagram reels, YouTube Shorts, Twitter, Facebook, your website or blog, LinkedIn, or even Pinterest. Do remember to adapt the content to suit the specific platform's requirements and audience preferences. You may need to adjust video format, captions, and descriptions to optimise engagement on each platform. I'll talk a little more about some of these areas in chapter 8.

As I mentioned in the introduction to this chapter, video has become an easy tool to use. All you need is your smartphone to show up, get noticed, and reach more people with your message. So there really is no excuse to not use video to market your business and your book!

Please do subscribe to my YouTube channel and watch some of the valuable videos on there – www.youtube.com/@librotas.

THINGS TO THINK ABOUT

There are many ways you can do video, from a 'live' on one of the social media platforms, to picking up your smartphone, doing a short piece to camera, or recording a professional video in a green screen studio.

As with any form of marketing, a consistent approach is important. If you choose to use video in your business, do it regularly.

There are plenty of ideas to choose from, so you could start with something short and build up to a longer form of video later on.

A great script, good lighting, and your smartphone are a good starting point to creating an effective video.

You need to grab people's attention from the moment they watch you, and remember to include a call to action that tells people what to do next.

_____

_____

_____

_____

_____

CHAPTER 7
Become a webinar whizz

Over the years, I have run countless webinars, online training, and masterclasses, using them as powerful tools to share valuable content. In this chapter, I will delve into the remarkable evolution of webinars, highlighting how they can help you to promote your business and your book.

When I first embarked on my entrepreneurial journey, teleclasses, teleseminars, and telesummits were all the rage. These typically involved conference calls where participants would dial in to listen to the knowledge imparted by the speakers. However, the advent of webinars changed the landscape entirely, transcending the limitations of a phone line. This shift opened up exciting possibilities, allowing participants to interact directly with speakers, ask questions, and express their thoughts through chat boxes.

Although I have been using Zoom and similar products for years, the impact of COVID-19 significantly transformed the webinar environment. One of the most popular questions on search engines in 2020 was, "How do I use Zoom?"

When physical gatherings and events were restricted, webinars became a powerful tool for connecting people across the globe. They have now become more than just a convenient way to disseminate information; they are now a vital platform for virtual collaboration, learning, and engagement.

As technology and functionality develops further, webinars have continued to evolve, embracing the convenience of on-demand access and evergreen approaches. These include pre-recorded global summits, challenges, and courses, often employing webinar software and incorporating various online training elements. Additionally, a spectrum of hybrid approaches has emerged, offering users the flexibility to consume information online, directly from the web. Undoubtedly, the future holds even more advancements and innovative technologies.

You might be asking whether webinars and online training should be prioritised among other media like blogging, podcasts, or videos. Well, there are unique advantages.

Firstly, webinars break down geographical barriers, allowing individuals from all corners of the globe to participate. This creates an opportunity to cultivate a worldwide audience that can learn about your expertise and engage with your book, without the need for physical travel.

Secondly, webinars enable you to deliver high-quality content to your clients at a relatively low cost. You can showcase your expertise and share valuable insights.

Thirdly, webinars can serve as compelling lead magnets, attracting individuals to join your mailing list when you offer free online training or masterclasses. And, when integrated into a paid-for programme, webinars become a highly effective vehicle for delivering rich and engaging content.

By leveraging webinars, you can seize the benefits of real-time engagement, offer valuable content, and create lasting assets that contribute to the growth of your business, while simultaneously enhancing your credibility as an expert author.

However, it is crucial to acknowledge that the immense popularity of webinars, much like any other content medium, has led to a discerning audience. To truly make an impact, you must strive to distinguish yourself by delivering exceptional information and high-quality training.

How to use webinars effectively

If you're wondering how you can use webinars effectively, here are some suggestions to inspire you.

Informational masterclasses: Host webinars where you teach valuable content and showcase your expertise. This approach works well when you're building your community and generating excitement about your upcoming book.

Valuable training: Share relevant and insightful content with your audience during webinars, and then leverage the opportunity to upsell to a product, programme, event, or even your book itself. This strategy allows you to deliver exceptional value whilst creating potential revenue streams.

Expert interviews: Collaborate with complementary experts in your field by conducting interview-style webinars. This not only adds value to both communities but also expands your reach to a wider audience. Additionally, these interviews can be repurposed into podcasts or videos for further content distribution.

Workshop, challenge, or training series: Develop a series of webinars that delve deep into specific topics related to your book. This can be a step-by-step workshop or a comprehensive training series where participants can learn actionable strategies and techniques. Consider offering these webinars for free or as part of a paid programme.

Panel discussion or roundtable event: Invite a panel of industry experts or fellow authors to join you in a webinar discussion. This format allows for diverse perspectives, stimulating conversations, and valuable insights. It also provides an opportunity to cross-promote each other's work and reach new audiences.

Q&A sessions: Dedicate a webinar session solely to answering audience questions. Encourage participants to submit their questions in advance or during the live session. This helps you to showcase your expertise while building a rapport with your audience.

Evergreen webinars: With evergreen webinars, you can pre-record your content and make it available for people to watch at their convenience. You have the flexibility to set it up as an on-demand experience or create the illusion of a real-time event using appropriate software. This approach allows you to reach a wider audience and generate continuous leads and engagement without scheduling constraints.

Book launch webinar: Host a webinar as a virtual book launch event. This allows you to engage with your audience, share insights about your book, read excerpts, and answer questions in real time. It creates a memorable and interactive experience for your readers, even if they can't attend a physical launch party.

As you can see, there is overlap with podcasts and video, but when you are smart about it, you can multipurpose and expand your content to reach different audiences with your content.

Don't let tech worries hold you back!

If you're new to running webinars, it's advisable to conduct practice sessions with trusted friends or colleagues before going live. This allows you to familiarise yourself with your preferred platform and iron out any potential issues.

Speaking from my own experience, I've encountered a variety of challenges, but they can be overcome with preparation and a positive mindset! Here are some scenarios I've faced:

I've been in situations where my internet has crashed or slowed down unexpectedly. It's important to have a backup plan in case of such disruptions, such as using a secondary internet connection or having a co-host who can take over if needed.

There have been instances where my internet simply refused to cooperate, forcing me to cancel a webinar. While it can be frustrating, it's essential to stay calm and communicate with your audience about the situation. You can always reschedule the webinar for another date.

It's easy to accidentally mute yourself during a webinar, leaving your audience unable to hear you! To avoid this, double-check your audio settings before starting, and consider using a headset to minimise background noise and improve audio quality.

During a live interview, I've had guests experience internet outages. In such cases, I have filled the time by engaging with the audience, sharing related insights. Flexibility and adaptability are key in managing unexpected circumstances.

It's not uncommon to forget to hit the record button, potentially missing out on capturing valuable content. To prevent this oversight, develop a habit of leaving yourself a visible reminder to record before each webinar.

There have also been occasions when I believed a webinar was successfully recorded, only to discover later that a system error occurred. It's advisable to periodically check your recording setup to ensure it is functioning correctly and consider alternative methods to record as a backup.

Remember, technical challenges can arise, but they should not discourage you. The best way to overcome them is through practice and hands-on experience.

Streamline and structure your topic

It is important to choose the topic of your webinar wisely, like you would do with any event, blog, or programme. Start with the end in mind. What do you want people to do after watching your webinar? For example, if you aim to upsell to an event, what do people need to know first? Then make sure your message is relevant. For example, don't run a webinar on '3 ways to manage stress at work' if you are promoting a programme on 'How to write a CV'.

When you start with the end in mind, it will help you to streamline your content, and work out what you're going to cover. Stick to three or four points, and make sure that you're providing content that your ideal readers are interested in hearing from you.

Think about how much content you can fit into your proposed time slot. As I've run so many webinars, I can pretty much gauge exactly how much content I need to cover in an hour and how many slides I need to deliver this. I'm normally spot on give or take a couple of minutes! If you're wondering how long your webinar should be, remember that people do have a limited attention span, so don't make it so long that people stop listening or switch off.

If you are using visuals, keep your slides to headlines, a few bullet points, and pictures. Include stories, case studies, and testimonials if they add value to your content and provide great social proof to back up any offers or promotions you might make during the webinar or afterwards. And if you are promoting a programme or product off the back of your webinar, sell the benefits and consider offering some bonuses as an incentive to take quick action.

On a practical note, it's important to know your material but not be too prescriptive. I like to have a few notes to keep me on track, as it's very easy to go off topic, especially if I am asked a question during the webinar and digress. The notes will bring me back to the content.

Engage your participants

One difference between running a webinar and a physical event is that it's not so easy to gauge the reactions of your audience, which may well faze some people. That's why it's really important to build connection early on with those on the call. Here are some strategies to engage your audience during webinars:

Poll insights: These provide a way to involve participants, make them feel included, and gain valuable insights that can enhance the webinar content.

Interactive exercises: Incorporating activities during your webinar will encourage active participation and engagement. For example, you can ask attendees to reflect on a question, solve a problem, or share their experiences in the chat box.

Q&A sessions: Allocate time for Q&A sessions. You can encourage attendees to ask questions via the question or chat box throughout the session and address them either in real time or at the end. This interaction not only allows for clarification but also enhances engagement by addressing their specific queries.

Chat box engagement: Encourage participants to use the chat box to share their thoughts, ideas, or provide feedback during the webinar. Regularly monitor the chat box and respond promptly to keep the conversation flowing and demonstrate your attentiveness to their needs.

Breakout rooms: If your webinar platform supports breakout rooms and you are running a more intimate webinar, you may consider breaking the participants into smaller groups for discussions or activities that allow them to connect with each other.

How to promote your webinar

The reason I haven't talked about promotion first is that you need to have an outline for your content before you create your sign-up page and promote your webinar. I'm going to be talking about sales pages in more detail in chapter 11, but here are some considerations to help you to promote your webinar.

Create a sign-up page: Develop a dedicated page for your webinar that provides detailed information about the event. Include compelling copy that highlights the benefits participants will gain from attending and a short but powerful biography that tells them why you are an expert in your topic. Make sure to include a clear call to action, such as a prominent sign-up button, to encourage registrations (remember AIDA?).

Promote it widely: There is a fine line between giving people too much notice and too little notice. I will generally start promoting a webinar 5–7 days before I run it. Promote it to your community, though I would advise sending a sequence of 3–5 emails, each focusing on a different angle related to your webinar, so people don't miss it or dismiss it. As well as promoting it to your community, share it on social media, your blog, podcasts, and videos. You can create engaging visuals, set up events on social media, do some social media advertising, and talk about it at every opportunity!

Reach out to other communities: In addition to promoting the webinar to your existing mailing list, consider reaching out to other relevant email lists or influencers in your industry. Collaborate with them to co-promote the webinar to their audience, expanding your reach and tapping into new networks. Be prepared to pay an affiliate commission if you're promoting a product or event off the back of your webinar.

Offer incentives: You could offer exclusive incentives to entice people to sign up and attend the live webinar. These could include downloadable resources, checklists, worksheets, e-book, or access to a limited-time offer. Highlight these incentives in your promotional materials to create a sense of urgency and value. You may also give people an incentive to attend live or not offer a recording!

Deliver your webinar and wow your audience

At this stage, I'll assume that you've created your content, developed your slides, and you've had people sign up for your webinar. I'll also assume that you've planned your promotion if applicable and have some stories and testimonials to share with your audience.

Here are a few practical reminders to make sure your webinar runs well:

Set up your environment where you will not be disturbed. Consider using a headset to avoid any background noise and warm up your voice first. Have a glass of water to hand and turn off your phone or any distractions.

Ensure that your webinar equipment is set up and functioning properly. Test your microphone, webcam, and screen-sharing capabilities before the webinar to avoid any technical issues. When you go live, conduct a quick audio and visual check to ensure that participants can hear you clearly and see any visual aids you plan to use.

Begin the webinar by welcoming participants and engaging them right from the start. You can ask a question, share an interesting fact, or deliver a brief overview of what they can expect during the session. This helps create a positive and interactive atmosphere from the beginning and allows you to settle into the webinar.

How to use webinars to promote your book

I'd like to end this chapter with some real-life examples of how I and some of my clients have used webinars to promote our businesses and books.

I ran a five-day Book Idea Challenge in January 2023. With daily live webinars, I delivered valuable content that enabled participants to connect with their book idea, explore different options, and engage with others who were in the early stages of their author's journey.

When Kate Barrett sought sponsorship for her book, one of the added bonuses she offered her sponsors were value-rich webinars that enabled her to showcase her expertise. More on this later in chapter 12.

Sarah Hamilton-Gill FCIPD is another great advocate for webinars. She has a tiered system. She delivers some webinars for free as lead magnets to build her list and some are chargeable, dependent on the content. Sarah also partners with people like me to add additional specialist value to her audience.

In May 2023, I participated as a speaker in the Ride the AI Wave Summit, which meant that I was able to get in front of a global audience alongside other speakers. Usually, when you participate on a summit like this, you will sign up to an agreement where you promote the event with your list and social media contacts as part of the arrangement, which means it's win-win for both parties, as they will actively promote it too.

I also have an evergreen webinar on my website which promotes the Smart Author System programme. This means that prospective authors can watch it at any time and find out how I can support them through the entire process of writing a book. I will touch on this further in chapter 19.

Whether you use Zoom or another piece of webinar software, whether you do it alone or partner with others, why not try it out and use webinars as part of your book marketing strategy!

 **THINGS TO THINK ABOUT**

Webinars, masterclasses, and other online trainings are great tools at any stage of your book's promotion, whether you want to build your community, sell your book, or promote a product or programme.

Test out the platforms before you get started or seek recommendations from your colleagues and friends. Before you go live, check your equipment and try it out in a safe environment first.

When developing your content, start with the end in mind. What do you want people to do after they've watched your webinar?

Keep your visuals simple – if you are using them – and don't cover too much content. Use stories and case studies to engage your audience.

Your webinars and training will become long-term assets. You might use recordings as bonuses later or include them as part of a bundle to enhance your reader's journey with you.

_____

_____

_____

_____

CHAPTER 8
Strategise with social media

Today, social media plays a crucial role for authors and publishers to help them reach a wider audience and create a solid author presence. Platforms such as Facebook, Twitter, Instagram, LinkedIn, and others offer you a unique opportunity to connect with readers, build your community, and promote your book.

As I mentioned in chapter 1, if you are seeking to go down the traditional publishing route, one of the things that a publisher will look for is great connections: a big list and many thousands of social media contacts. If you are going down the partnership or independent publishing route, it's also important to have a strong following on social media if this is where your readers hang out. Not only can you use them to raise the profile of your book, they will also raise the profile of your business.

In this chapter, I will explore how you can harness the power of social media strategically using these four platforms to enhance your book marketing efforts. It's important to note that social media isn't a standalone tool and is a really good way to complement the other suggestions already offered to you in this book.

But first, let me share some strategies that are pretty much generic to any platform you use.

Choose the right social media platforms: Choose the right social media platform or platforms that are likely to appeal to your target reader and then tailor your messages accordingly. Each social media platform offers unique benefits for book marketing. Facebook provides a broad reach and targeted advertising options. Twitter's fast-paced nature is ideal for quick updates and engaging in conversations. Instagram's visual appeal is perfect for showcasing book covers and behind-the-scenes moments. LinkedIn caters to a professional audience, making it one of the best platforms for non-fiction business authors.

Develop your social media strategy: Take some time to set some goals for your book. What is the purpose of your social media presence? Do you want to increase book sales, build brand awareness, or connect with influencers? Plan your content strategically, including key dates, holidays, book-related events, or other promotions. You can explore engagement tactics such as giveaways and contests to engage your audience.

Create a strong first impression: When creating your social media profile, choose a professional profile picture that reflects your personal image. Next, write a compelling biography that concisely captures your expertise. Use keywords and relevant hashtags to highlight your niche and make it easier for others to find you. And don't forget to craft your banner or cover photo with visually appealing imagery that aligns with your brand or showcases your personality.

Create engaging content: Like with any form of marketing, you need to capture your readers' attention on social media. Here are some examples: author interviews, behind-the-scenes glimpses into your author journey, book excerpts, quotes, book trailers, and interactive posts. Visuals, videos, and infographics can enhance engagement and make your posts stand out. It's worth experimenting with different formats to see what resonates with your audience, and what they engage with the most. And don't forget to include a call to action, so people know what to do next, whether this is to comment on your post, answer a question, sign up for your mailing list or buy your book!

Interact and engage: It's important to mention that social media success isn't just about sharing your own content, it's also about responding to other people's posts, resharing interesting content, replying promptly to comments, messages and reviews, initiating conversations, and encouraging discussions. By nurturing meaningful connections with your audience, you can turn readers into fans and generate buzz around your book.

Track and analyse results: It makes sense to measure the effectiveness of your social media efforts, so schedule in time to track your metrics. Use social media analytics tools to monitor engagement, reach, click-through rates, and conversions. You will gain insights into which content performs well and identify areas for improvement.

Don't rely solely on social media: Let me remind you that it's crucial to encourage people to join your mailing list. This means you can retain control over your communication channels, as this safeguards your business from potential disruptions.

Now let me delve into the four core platforms with a brief summary of what to expect with some experts I have worked with who can help you.

Twitter thoughts

Initially launched in 2006, Twitter started out as a micro blogging platform that allowed users to share short, 140-character tweets. Although users can now write longer updates, it still focuses on short and succinct updates.

With around 400 million users globally and 259.4 million daily active users[1], Twitter is a fast-paced platform and a great place to connect with like-minded individuals.

Hashtags play a significant role on Twitter. When posting your content, think about your hashtags as they can help increase the visibility of your tweets and connect with those interested in your content. Industry or business-specific hashtags or writing hashtags such as #amwriting #businessbooks #lovewriting and #writingcommunity are popular in the author community.

It is also a place where agents, publishers, and industry professionals hang out. You can stay informed about the latest trends and by engaging in industry conversations you can gain visibility and establish yourself as a knowledgeable author. You can also participate in writing discussions, join writing communities, and connect with fellow authors. You can use hashtags to find relevant discussions.

Many journalists are active on Twitter, using it as a platform to interact with their audience. You can engage by sharing their tweets or giving your insights on relevant topics. Journalists also use Twitter to seek experts for stories, so keep an eye on hashtags such as #journorequests for the latest opportunities to contribute to articles or respond to press requests. As a result of #journorequests, I have been featured in numerous publications including the *Daily Mail* and the *Daily Express*.

Twitter is also a great way to connect with potential endorsers. When I wanted an influential entrepreneur to write the foreword for my second book, *How to Stand Out in your Business*, I approached Rachel Elnaugh (formerly of *Dragons' Den* and Red Letter Days). I knew she was prolific on Twitter, so I sent her a short tweet and this resulted in a great testimonial for my book!

One thing I like about Twitter is that you can set up lists to keep an eye on those who are influential or interesting. In a nutshell, if you choose to use Twitter as a core promotional tool, share great content, follow and engage, build relationships, and show up regularly!

Facebook fans

Facebook is a social networking site founded in 2004. With billions of active users worldwide, it is best known as a hub for connecting with friends, family, and colleagues. Users can create personal profiles, join groups, follow pages, and share content as text posts, photos, and videos. Facebook is often seen as a place where people are more likely to share their dinner and personal pursuits, and many people fail to realise how useful Facebook can be to business and their book.

A personal profile is a great starting point as you can connect with your friends and business contacts, and share relevant information on your page. It is important to note that Facebook prefers you to have a business page to promote business-related news, though I do share some business news on my personal profile. If you're worried about your business connections getting to know your personal business, then you can set lists to manage your privacy settings.

I advise that you also have a business page for your business. This allows you to share information about your business and your book and build a community of people who love what you do. You can share book reviews, give away snippets, create events, and give updates and tips to those who like your page, though the Facebook algorithms mean that only a few of your fans will see your posts.

You can join Facebook groups related to your business and book topic. While you'll need to bear in mind the rules of the group, they can be great places to participate in discussions, share insights, ask questions, answer questions, connect with others and, if permitted, tell people about your new book.

You can also host your own groups. I have a public 'Author's Journey' Facebook group and private Facebook groups for clients and members of my programmes. These are great spaces to ask questions, voice concerns, and celebrate successes. You could offer something similar for your own programmes or for people who have bought your book.

As I mentioned in my general social media tips, I advise posting useful content regularly to keep people engaged and informed. On Facebook you can add video, photos, and graphics to make your posts interesting and stand out. Videos have been particularly popular in recent years. Not only can you share carefully curated videos, but you can also go live on a page, in a group, or on your personal profile to share tips, stories, or anything you like!

Lastly, you may consider Facebook advertising via your business page. These allow you to reach a wider audience for your book or lead magnet as you can target ads to specific demographics, interests, or geographical locations.

LinkedIn linkups

LinkedIn launched in 2003 and is the oldest social media platform. It's a great tool to develop professional relationships online. You can establish a professional presence, network with industry peers, and showcase your expertise.

You will hear from Alice Fewings shortly with some of her tips to get noticed on LinkedIn, but first I'd like to share some stats she shared with me that are correct as of 2023:

- There are currently 950 million LinkedIn users worldwide[2]
- 80% of B2B leads on social media come from LinkedIn[3]
- According to Hubspot 2023, LinkedIn is 277% more effective at generating leads than Facebook and Twitter[4]

LinkedIn is one of my favourite social media platforms and that's because it can give you huge scope to establish yourself as a thought leader.

You can start by crafting your compelling profile that highlights your professional achievements and expertise with a concise and engaging headline that communicates your value and mentions you are an author!

You can share valuable content related to your book's topics or business insights through LinkedIn articles or regular posts, and position yourself as a thought leader by providing industry-specific knowledge, insights, and practical tips. You can engage in discussions within relevant LinkedIn groups, demonstrating your expertise and contributing to the professional community.

I like to connect with those I have met at networking events, and to search and connect with potential endorsers, influencers, or collaborators. You can also request recommendations and endorsements from colleagues, clients, or readers who have benefited from your expertise, which can help build trust and credibility.

If you have written articles, white papers, or reports related to your non-fiction book's topics, you can consider publishing them on LinkedIn's publishing platform. And you can use the publications section to feature your book.

Remember to actively engage with your LinkedIn connections by commenting on their posts, sharing relevant content, and participating in industry discussions. Regularly updating your LinkedIn profile with your latest accomplishments, speaking engagements, or media coverage helps to maintain a strong professional presence.

I have asked LinkedIn expert Alice Fewings to share some additional strategies with you to help you get noticed on LinkedIn.

FIVE WAYS TO GET NOTICED ON LINKEDIN BY ALICE FEWINGS

The last decade has seen some radical changes in the way we use social media platforms, and LinkedIn hasn't been left behind. Like the other social platforms, it's changed and adapted to suit the needs of its users.

When I first set up my LinkedIn profile I never would have dreamed of creating and sharing vulnerable content about my thoughts, feelings, and experiences. This style of content would have felt far too personal for LinkedIn and a world away from the polished content I once thought the platform expected.

But now, things are different. Showing up authentically and connecting is what is most favoured by both the algorithm and the platform users.

Right now you have such an opportunity to show up with content in the newsfeed, to get noticed and to build fruitful business relationships. And it all starts with standing out in saturated newsfeed and drawing the attention of your ideal audience.

Did you know that you have, on average, 13 milliseconds to grab someone's attention from the newsfeed? That's it! That's the rate people are scrolling and how long they'll spare to glance at your content. So, something needs to make your post stand out.

And I'll let you in on a LinkedIn secret... nothing will stand out more than you.

Here are 5 ways that you can confidently show up with content and get noticed on LinkedIn:

1. **Be recognisable:** Your audience will stop on your post when they can instantly recognise it's you, whether that's in the branding or the photos (this means it's time to take some selfies!).

2. **Be memorable:** Position yourself as the go-to industry expert that you are and be consistent with your key messages.

3. **Be personable:** To connect with you your audience need to see themselves in your story. So, use your content to talk about what matters to you, what you did at the weekend and what you're celebrating right now. Use your posts to spark authentic connection.

4. **Be varied:** Create an equal amount of content that educates, inspires, sparks conversations, connects, and promotes your products or services. Set yourself up as the go-to industry expert that people know, like, and trust — this is where the magic happens!

5. **Be a storyteller:** Bring people on a journey with you. It can make all the difference.

Keep showing up on LinkedIn for your audience, be social, and build those professional relationships because people will love to get to know and work with YOU.

Alice Fewings is an award-winning LinkedIn trainer and coach, empowering entrepreneurs to reach new audiences, raise their profile, and attract more clients. Visit www.alicefewings.com.

Instagram inspiration

Last, and by no means least, let's talk about Instagram. With over 1.6 billion users worldwide[5], and half a billion of these using stories every day, engagement rates on Instagram are typically higher than on other social media platforms.

Instagram's visually appealing nature makes it an ideal platform for you to showcase your book, build a community of readers, and establish a strong author brand. By leveraging Instagram effectively, you can connect with your audience on a more personal level. You can visually showcase your book, share behind-the-scenes moments, and provide glimpses into your writing process.

Using high-quality images, graphics, and videos you can tell compelling stories related to your book's topics or your author journey. You can curate a visually appealing grid by maintaining a consistent aesthetic, colour scheme, or theme that aligns with your brand and book.

I have asked Karen Duncan to share her tips to help you to master Instagram.

 THREE WAYS TO MASTER INSTAGRAM BY KAREN DUNCAN

Instagram is a very visual platform, but that doesn't mean you can't promote books. There are handy features that can help you connect to readers in almost any niche.

1. Show your expertise

Instagram uses pictures and video, both of which can show you know your onions. You could use #ThrowbackThursday to show your graduation, starting your business, or a key point in your life. You can use video to explain handy and short tips: reels work best under a minute as it's long enough to give valuable information, but short enough to easily absorb.

Instagram likes it if you post regularly. This doesn't have to be every day but if you post a couple of times a week and keep this up, you will find your audience growing. If you link your Facebook and Instagram accounts, you can use Business Suite on Facebook to schedule. The most useful thing about this is once you have more than 50 followers, it will tell you the best time to post. This makes sure your audience sees your updates.

2. Check your hashtags

You may be familiar with hashtags on other platforms to let people know the themes in your post. This is how new people will find you as you can follow hashtags or search for ones of interest.

Instagram hashtags have far more variation – you could, for instance, describe a female business owner as #bossbabe, #entrepreneur, #womaninbiz and many others. Chances are there is one that appeals most. You can search for hashtags on www.displaypurposes.com to create a list. Copy and paste three to five of the most relevant at the end of the post and alternate, making sure you reach slightly different people each time.

3. Use Instagram Stories

Stories appear in circles at the top of your feed. They are posts that disappear after 24 hours but have useful features. You can add these to stories by looking at Stickers – the smiley square at the top. Countdowns can be used to remind people how long is left on a kickstarter or when to buy launch tickets. Links can take them exactly to where they can sign up, or to your blogs or podcasts.

You can also use Stories as permanent highlights on your profile – click on the circle with the plus sign above your grid to keep these useful links easy to find.

Instagram takes some perseverance, but you can create a great impression using these tips and your creativity. Good luck!

Karen Duncan is a social media marketing trainer helping small businesses stand out online through short courses and consultations. PonyPonyPony Courses can be found at: www.ponyponypony.co.uk.

What to post on social media

When you've decided your best approach on social media, it's time to decide how to use them most effectively. I touched on this briefly in the introduction to this chapter and here are some other things you can do:

Tell people about your book: This is the most obvious thing to do. Give your subscribers regular updates, give them a chance to read a snippet, and share your highs and lows.

Ask for contributions to your book: If you are looking for other experts to contribute to your book, like I've done in this one, using your social media contacts is a great way to do this.

Share your blogs, videos, and podcasts: This enables you to reach more people with the content you have curated and make a bigger impact with your potential readers.

Turn your wisdom into pictures: Tools such as Canva have made it much easier to turn your written word into visual pictures, reels, or stories that you can share online. Many tools like this have free or low-cost versions that you can use, although this may give you limited functionality. You could simply take your own quotes and tips from your blog or your book and use these tools to create them. Add your name and web address onto them, which will be shared when they go viral.

Turn other people's quotes into pictures: If you don't yet have your own quotes or tips to share (although I'd question this!), you can use other people's quotes that are in the public domain. Remember to attribute the quote to the right person, and add your web address or logo.

Share your top tips: You don't have to put your quotes into pictures. You could simply type them into Twitter, Facebook, etc and share them with your followers. These would be short and sweet snippets and you could finish by adding a call to action driving traffic towards your book.

Share reviews and tell people how they can buy your book: Once you've published your book, share reviews, as other people's opinions will help sell your book without you needing to promote it.

Tell your followers about other updates: You could also share other things that you're doing. For example, LinkedIn is a great place to tell people what you're up to each day, and you can share information like your next speaking engagement, media coverage, videos of you speaking about your book, podcast interviews, or other relevant information.

Link in with notable days or events: Keep an eye on specific days or events that link in with your book content and write valuable content that you can share online.

Comment on news: If there are newsworthy topics linked to your book, create a post with your take on the topic and share with your audience.

How to make social media simple

Many social media platforms allow you to schedule your posts in advance, or you can use a social media scheduling tool if you prefer. Live interaction is always preferable but scheduled content is better than nothing!

Batch create your content in advance, so you don't have to think on the hoof about what you want to share. You may decide to share tips on one day of the week, a blog post on a different day of the week; it's really up to you.

Although I've not tried this myself, you could use a tool like ChatGPT to turn content previously produced in a different form, such as a blog or a video script, into social media content that could promote it.

If you're wondering how often to post, then most social media experts suggest posting four times a week, but once a week is better than nothing!

Even though this information is in the pre-launch part of this book, this is something that you need to be doing regularly. Consistent content will help you to build your contacts, likes and followers, and as you develop your book, you'll develop more specific content that you can target towards your ideal readership.

Social media platforms give you a great way to reach more people with your book, but they do take time to build – and they can be a time suck if you're not careful!

THINGS TO THINK ABOUT

Social media is a great way of reaching new people and connecting with those who you've already met. It's not just about telling people how they can buy your book, it's about sharing valuable information and showing up as a thought leader.

Use the social media platforms where your clients hang out and post regularly on topics that will interest them.

Consider how you can use social media platforms to also engage with potential influencers, endorsers, and partners.

Although you can schedule posts and updates, real-time interaction will better engage your audience.

Use your time wisely, otherwise you'll never finish writing your book!

_____

_____

_____

_____

_____

_____

CHAPTER 9
Cultivate your connections

Networking is a powerful tool that allows us to forge meaningful connections, unlock opportunities, and expand our horizons. In today's interconnected world, the concept of 'six degrees of separation' serves as a reminder of the remarkable ties that bind us. It suggests that any two individuals, no matter how far apart they may seem, can be connected through a chain of acquaintances spanning just six degrees of separation. This idea highlights the immense potential of our social networks and the vast web of relationships that surround us.

In this chapter, I will explore the art of networking and delve into strategies for leveraging these connections to build mutually beneficial relationships. When you engage in conversations regularly, you can open the doors to unexpected opportunities and connections that can elevate your business and book's success.

From formal networking opportunities to informal networking and online events, I will consider effective strategies for making lasting impressions and crafting compelling elevator pitches. I'll touch on the importance of finding the right networking groups and consistently attending them to establish familiarity and trust.

This chapter also considers the follow-up process, which is often overlooked. I will provide practical guidance on how to nurture connections through email, social media, and professional platforms, ensuring that mutually beneficial relationships are maintained and cultivated.

Finally, I will consider the importance of joint venture partnerships and speaking opportunities as effective strategies to establish yourself as an expert in your field. By collaborating with complementary businesses and sharing your expertise through speaking engagements, you can enhance your visibility and connect with individuals who need to hear your message.

Create networking opportunities

To develop your connections, networking with others is a great starting point, as you get to talk with people. The lack of real conversation is one of the downsides of social media in my opinion. When you can talk with people, you can tell them about your book ideas and get their feedback. Most importantly it's a great opportunity to find out about them, and build a relationship which is mutually beneficial.

When I talk about networking, this includes formal networking opportunities and events where you may share your 60-second elevator pitch. It also includes informal opportunities such as events, expos and conferences where you may have conversations over a cup of coffee or even in the toilet queue! And I also include online networking where you may pop into breakout rooms and engage with other like-minded individuals.

It's important to note here that, as a result of the COVID-19 pandemic, it became commonplace to hold and attend networking events online, and even three-plus years on, many of us have embraced the convenience of virtual networking. It certainly saves travel time and it's opened up the world as we network globally without having to jump into the car or get a train.

However you network, it is important to have a short introduction that grabs people's attention, as well as having a longer elevator pitch that can be varied depending on the rules of the networking group. You might want to tell a story, give examples of how you work, and have some sort of call to action so that the listener knows how they can approach you for more information. But remember, when you're having conversations, we do have two ears and one mouth for a reason! Keep in mind actively listening to others rather than just talking about you.

Most people who are successful in business do networking on some level, whether they choose to go to larger events or workshops, or attend local networking groups. If you're not doing some sort of networking, then you're definitely missing out. As well as spending time with others – a must if you're working on your own – it gives you the chance to meet new people. If you find networking a struggle, perhaps you've not yet found the right one for you, as different groups work for different people. Once you've found one that works, however, attend on a regular basis so that people can get to know you.

The purpose of networking isn't to sell. Not in my eyes anyway. The purpose is to build relationships, have conversations, and this may later lead to a new client or a referral. Remember if you're in a room of 40 people, you're not just talking to those 40 people; you're also talking to their contacts who may need your help.

Due to my own networks, it's not unusual for someone I know to connect me with other people I can help and vice versa. On a personal level, many of the people I now work with as colleagues were once people I met through networking events. I've referred people who now work with each other, and I've recommended people to connect, and being able to help others is important to business – and book – success.

I asked Caroline Andrew-Johnstone, Managing Director of 4Networking, to share some of her tips with you.

FIVE TIPS TO MAXIMISE YOUR NETWORKING OPPORTUNITIES BY CAROLINE ANDREW-JOHNSTONE

Building business relationships from networking is a continuous process. From the moment you meet someone new you need to have a plan in place to capitalise on the opportunities, both for yourself and your networking partners. So, here are 5 things to keep in mind at every networking opportunity.

1. Networking should be 80% of your marketing activity, and everywhere there are networking opportunities. Your pitch needs to be perfect and ready to roll out whenever you get the chance. Think about what problem you solve for potential customers, have evidence of how you do it, a testimonial perhaps.

2. Perfect your listening skills. Tune in to what others are saying in their pitches and think about how you can help them. Turn off distractions. These include your phone and emails if you are in an online meeting, and the negative voice that is thinking about the other ways you could be spending the time.

3. Meeting someone at a networking meeting, online, or in person, is only the start. The real relationship building begins now. Get contact details and follow up so you can learn more about each other's businesses.

4. Have what the networking experts call your 'referral radar' on at all times. Do you know someone who could help solve a problem for your new connection? Being a trusted partner and referrer will get you noticed. People have built entire businesses out of doing just that.

5. Play the longer game. You will be in business for years, and so will your connections. The time may not be right to work

together now, but it will be at some point in the future. Keep in touch on LinkedIn, at meetings, and through emails and phone calls. But don't spam them; that is the quick way to destroy a potential partnership.

There is of course so much more to networking than these simple tips. Author, speaker, and networking guru Jim Rohn said: "The fortune is in the follow up." If you take away only that from reading these tips, then you will have improved your chances of building business through networking many times over.

Caroline Andrew-Johnstone is the Networking Rebel and managing director of 4Networking, the UK's largest joined-up network, which offers in-person and online networking opportunities. Find out more at www.4nonline.biz.

Online networking

It would be remiss of me not to touch on online networking in more detail, as it has emerged as a powerful complement to traditional face-to-face networking.

Whilst face-to-face networking allows for personal interactions and immediate rapport-building, online networking offers the ability to connect with individuals from diverse geographical locations. You can engage with others at any time of the day and night and in multiple time zones. These groups have brought together like-minded individuals who share common interests, industries, or goals.

Another difference between physical and online networking is the mode of communication. In face-to-face networking, we rely on verbal and non-verbal cues to convey messages and build connections and trust. These cues facilitate a deeper understanding and trust between individuals. In contrast, online networking primarily only allows you to share a limited part of your body, which may lack the nuances of non-verbal cues. As a result, building trust and establishing genuine connections may require additional effort.

Despite these differences, the fundamental principles of networking remain consistent across physical and online contexts. Actively listening, showing genuine interest in others, and seeking opportunities to provide value and support are essential strategies for successful networking. And, of course, remembering to take yourself off mute is one of the biggest learnings that many of us have faced!

The fortune is in the follow-up

Whilst initial interactions and networking events serve as valuable starting points, it is the follow-up that solidifies relationships, uncovers opportunities, and builds long-term connections. It allows you to continue the conversation, exchange information, and explore potential partnerships.

Whether you reach out via email, connect with LinkedIn, or pick up the telephone, you can nurture the relationship and keep yourself at the forefront of your contacts' minds. Or you can meet your contact for a physical or 'virtual' coffee to continue the relationship.

Develop joint venture partnerships

Let's bring this chapter back to your book. Networking allows you to meet more people and the more people you connect with the more people who can support you at all stages of your book's creation and launch.

Joint venture partnerships can be a powerful strategy to promote your book effectively. By forming alliances with complementary businesses or influential individuals, you can leverage your partner's existing audience, expertise, and marketing channels to expand the reach of your book.

But it's not just about you; joint ventures provide an opportunity for strategic collaboration, where both parties can benefit from increased visibility, credibility, and revenue generation.

Whether you have a formal arrangement or informal collaboration, by combining resources, such as cross-promoting content through your respective mailing lists, or organising joint events, you can create a synergy that maximises exposure and creates a win-win situation for all involved.

For example, I occasionally work with partners to help promote the Smart Author System programme. I will run a webinar with the partner, and they may receive a commission for anyone who signs up for the programme as a thank you. I've also worked with partners on podcasts and summits. I've had some wonderful people support me with this book and many have also added huge value to my Smart Author membership community by providing valuable content in the form of interviews for members.

Remember, collaborations can enable you to reach new audiences, increase book sales, gain credibility through working with reputable partners and expand your professional network.

Seek speaking opportunities

I've included my tips on speaking in chapter 20 in the post-launch phase, but equally you may find that this is a good strategy before you launch your book.

Like networking, it is a good way to connect with people who need to hear your message, and a great way to showcase your expertise. If you do seek speaking opportunities at this stage, it is a good way to find out what your readers want to hear before you've published it, and there's nothing stopping you from pre-selling your book before it's even finished!

Many networking organisations have speaking opportunities for members, so why not volunteer your services to get you started, which will allow you to showcase your expertise.

 **THINGS TO THINK ABOUT**

Make sure that networking is part of your book marketing strategy, whether you attend formal events or have informal meetings.

Remember that networking is a two-way thing. What can you do to help others in your network? What referral or other opportunities may benefit them?

Consider your elevator pitch and introduction, so that when someone asks you about what you do, you have a strong and clear answer.

Building your community is not just about getting readers for your books and new clients, it's also about developing relationships and getting feedback.

Consider different types of joint venture partners who may be advantageous for your book and where you may be able to find the perfect people to support you.

_____

_____

_____

_____

_____

CHAPTER 10
Receive rave reviews and rally your street team

Once you've got your networking in place and have built your connections, it's time to expand your book's audience and get influential endorsements, which is what I will explore in this chapter.

There are four key areas I will be covering:

Peer reviews, which are invaluable as you approach the final manuscript stage to offer valuable feedback, insights, and critical perspectives on your manuscript.

I will explore the benefits of engaging ARC (Advance Reader Copy) reviewers who receive advance copies of your book in exchange for honest feedback. These reviewers play a vital role in generating early buzz and word-of-mouth recommendations.

Additionally, to increase your book's visibility and credibility, endorsements from well-known figures or experts can lend authority and attract potential readers.

Lastly, I will focus on the importance of building a passionate street team. This group of dedicated supporters actively promotes your book, spreading the word within their networks and participating in promotional activities. Their enthusiasm and advocacy can significantly contribute to the success of your book launch.

Peer reviewers: get valuable insights

Before you rush to publish your manuscript, it is crucial to seek feedback from others. Peer reviewers play a vital role in providing valuable insights before the editing stage. It's important to note that when you send your book for peer reviews, it won't be perfect yet and this step helps you identify any issues before you have your book professionally edited and published. It's also important to note that it's not unusual to have your finger over the send button for many hours before you hit the button, as it can be nerve-racking to send it out for peer review feedback!

I suggest you choose reviewers from your network who can provide balanced feedback, avoiding close friends or family members who may be less objective. These peer reviewers should ideally be familiar with your niche or your book's goals. They may be clients or former clients, business colleagues, or even members of your team. You may also ask your social media contacts to come forward and help you. I've done this more than once to get unbiased peer reviews for some of my books from people who don't know me.

Their feedback should focus on highlighting what they love about your book, addressing areas for improvement, and critically evaluating the information, rather than proofreading for spelling and grammar errors. You do, however, need to take on board any constructive feedback, as this will ultimately improve your manuscript, but remember that you have the final say regarding edits or changes.

You might also be wondering how this links in with marketing. Well, alongside asking your peer reviewers to give you constructive feedback on your book, you might ask them to write a short review for you, which you can use in the 'praise' section in the front of your book alongside any influencer reviews. You can also use these reviews on marketing material, sales pages, and other promotional content with their permission.

ARC reviewers: generate buzz and feedback

Once you have incorporated feedback from peer reviewers and made necessary changes, you might consider engaging ARC reviewers. These reviewers are individuals who receive early access to your book before its official release.

Unlike peer reviewers, ARC reviewers are typically not acquainted with you personally. Their primary role is to help generate excitement and create a buzz around your book before its launch. ARC reviewers provide feedback directly to the author or publisher and may share their thoughts on social media or related forums to promote your book. The inclusion of ARC reviewers alongside peer reviewers adds a fresh perspective to the feedback you receive. They may be asked to share their thoughts about your book with their followers, social media, or on related forums to create a buzz for your book.

To find ARC reviewers, check out book bloggers within your niche. You can check out their website to see if they accept submissions. Explore online communities focused on book reviews, such as Goodreads, Reedsy, and NetGalley. These platforms often have dedicated sections for authors seeking reviewers. Create an author account, participate in relevant discussions, and connect with potential reviewers who have similar reading interests.

When reaching out to potential ARC reviewers, always be professional, and transparent about your expectations and timelines. Offer them a free digital copy of your book and ask for their feedback and review within a reasonable timeframe before the official book launch.

You might now be wondering if you need both peer reviewers and ARCs in place, and this does depend upon your timescales and goals for your book. In my view, peer reviewers are essential as they provide critical feedback from those you trust, whereas ARC reviewers tend to be used by traditional publishers who already have established relationships with reviewers, bloggers, and industry influencers, and are less likely to be used for niche business books. However there are advantages: your ARC reviewers don't know you, so this can add a different dynamic to the feedback you receive.

Influential endorsers: add credibility to your book

Consider having influential endorsers to add valuable credibility to your book, especially if they are well respected in your industry or niche. Endorsers contribute valuable social proof and can position you as an expert in your field, ultimately increasing your book's visibility.

Endorsers can be authors, experts, celebrities, leaders, or other influential individuals known and respected in your book's niche. Their endorsements can build credibility and generate interest among potential readers. Although there may be some overlap between ARC reviewers and endorsers, it's important to recognise the distinct roles they play.

To get access to endorsers and influencers needs patience and perseverance. Reaching out to people you don't already know can be challenging but not impossible. I always recommend that you start by identifying people who might be a good fit for endorsing your book. They are likely to be well known in your field or by your readers. Look for those with significant social media followings or those who have endorsed similar books in the past.

Begin by considering people you already know who might be appropriate, then leverage social media platforms, search engines, or online forums to discover additional individuals. For example, you can reach out to them directly via social media channels, their agents, or their publishers. Or use your own contacts to find someone with a connection to this person. Explain why you believe their endorsement would be valuable and offer to send them an advance copy of your book for review. If you don't receive a response initially, follow up respectfully, remaining persistent without being pushy. Regardless of the outcome, always express gratitude for their time and consideration.

Endorsers for my past books have included Rachel Elnaugh, formerly on *Dragons' Den*, who (as I mentioned earlier) I reached out to on Twitter. I asked Peter Thomson to write the foreword for my first book when I attended one of his events. Gladeana McMahon, formerly the chair of the Association for Coaching and one of my experts in my first book, wrote the foreword for the first edition of this book and I approached Karen Skidmore, one of my trusted business mentors, to pen the foreword for this second edition. Motivational speaker Brian Tracy endorsed my first book and life coach, author, and former *Psychologies* editor Suzy Walker reviewed *The Mouse That Roars*.

For my clients, their success has been reaching into their network to find out who they know and who knows the people they want to know and then asking for an introduction. They have attracted endorsements from well-known experts like top business coach and owner of Action Coach® Brad Sugars, Brad Burton (known as the UK's number one motivational speaker), MP Jess Phillips, TV personality Victoria Derbyshire, musician Fatboy Slim, CEOs of international organisations, renowned academics, sports personalities, bestselling authors, and motivational speakers.

However, your reviewers don't all need to be well-known individuals; you can also reach out to your clients, colleagues, and social media followers to seek their endorsement for your book.

Street team: get ready for your launch

In recent years, the concept of creating a street team has gained popularity. This team consists of passionate supporters who assist in promoting your book to a wider audience, including their own networks and communities. Street team members may have a personal connection to you, such as being part of your mailing list or social media following, or they may simply resonate with your message.

They play a crucial role in promoting your book on social media, leaving reviews on platforms like Amazon or Goodreads, and recommending your book to their friends and colleagues. In exchange for their support, provide exclusive or early access to content or a digital copy of your book, bonus incentives, and other rewards that align with their contributions.

When establishing your street team, clearly communicate your expectations and desired actions, including specific timelines. It is likely you will ask them to register to receive information from you, which might be a form on your website where you can capture their contact details. This allows you to easily provide them with the necessary assets, such as links to relevant content, images, and promotional materials with the web links, to make their promotional efforts seamless.

I suggest you set clear guidelines for participation, provide them with enough time to be able to help you and maintain regular communication to ensure everyone is on track. Ensure you appreciate their efforts and recognise their contributions to your book's success – you may decide to offer an additional gift to those who have supported you with your launch, such as a complimentary programme or other incentive.

Next steps

Like all the strategies in this book, don't try and do everything or at least not all at once, but reaching out to your networks and their connections will hugely impact upon the success of your book. By yourself, you have a limited reach, and you need to reach more people who are interested in your message and ready to buy your book.

The need for peer reviewers, ARC reviewers, endorsements, and a street team will depend upon your individual goals, your book topic, your ideal readership, and your book marketing strategy, so consider what is most important to your book's launch. It will also depend upon the timescales you have available and the resources at your disposal to make this happen.

As with any form of marketing, do a couple of things well rather than spreading yourself too thinly. There is a reason why this chapter appears now. Once you already have your website, content, and community building in place as you write your book, then you will have established your presence and this bit can be implemented during the editing phase of your book!

 **THINGS TO THINK ABOUT**

Seek feedback from trusted peer reviewers before publishing your book, as they provide valuable insights and can help you identify areas for improvement.

Influential endorsers add credibility and weight to your book. Identify individuals within your industry or niche who can vouch for your work.

ARC reviewers can generate buzz and provide fresh perspectives. Consider engaging them alongside peer reviewers to further refine your book.

Building a street team empowers passionate supporters to promote your book. Clarify expectations, provide resources, and maintain regular communication with your team.

Customise your approach to fit your individual goals, book topic, readership, and available resources.

_____

_____

_____

_____

_____

CHAPTER 11
Pre-sell before publishing

Alongside getting reviews and endorsements for your book, it's time to consider putting some other strategies in place to promote your book ready for launch. In this chapter, I am going to cover the concept of pre-selling your book.

I know, the idea of selling a book before it's even published might seem scary at first. But fear not! I will be exploring some practical strategies to help you secure pre-orders and lay the groundwork for a successful book launch, without overwhelming you.

Pre-selling your book has a multitude of benefits. It not only enables you to create early buzz around your work but can also provide the financial boost you need to cover any publishing and marketing costs and may lead to some early media coverage. It can serve as a powerful motivator to finish writing that masterpiece you've been pouring your heart and soul into. All of this will pave the way for a successful launch!

Let's start this chapter by delving deeper into each point:

Creating a buzz early: Pre-selling your book allows you to generate excitement and anticipation among your target audience before your publication date. By announcing the availability of pre-orders, you're signalling that something special is on its way. This early buzz can generate curiosity and intrigue, capturing the attention of readers who are eager to be among the first to experience your work. This heightened interest can result in increased visibility for your book, as readers share their anticipation with others, both online and offline. Word-of-mouth marketing will kick up a gear, as you spread the news of your upcoming release.

Generating income for publishing and marketing: Pre-selling offers a practical solution for authors who may have budget constraints but still aspire to publish and market their book effectively. By securing pre-orders, you can generate revenue that can be allocated towards various publishing expenses, such as cover design, editing, formatting, and printing. Furthermore, having financial resources from pre-orders empowers you to invest in marketing initiatives to create a broader reach for your book. It provides you with the necessary funds to run promotional campaigns, leverage social media advertising, or engage in other marketing activities that boost visibility and drive more sales.

Potential media coverage: When you have a substantial number of pre-orders and early buzz surrounding your book, you increase the likelihood of attracting media attention. Journalists, bloggers, and podcasters are often interested in stories that are generating excitement and capturing the interest of readers. By leveraging your pre-orders as a hook, you can pitch your book to various media outlets and increase your chances of securing interviews, reviews, features, or mentions. This media exposure not only expands your book's reach but also enhances your credibility as an author, creating a positive cycle of increased visibility and further pre-orders.

Serving as a powerful motivator: Pre-selling your book provides a compelling incentive and sense of accountability to complete the writing process. Knowing that readers are eagerly waiting to get their hands on your book can serve as a powerful motivator to stay committed, focused, and disciplined during the writing journey. The anticipation and support from pre-orders will validate the importance of your writing, fuelling your determination to deliver a masterpiece that lives up to readers' expectations. The act of pre-selling not only generates external motivation but also reinforces your own belief in the value of your book. Ultimately, the journey of pre-selling can be the catalyst that propels you toward the finish line, turning your book dreams into a reality.

Buy your book's website domain

The first step in preparing for the pre-selling journey is securing a dedicated website domain for your book. Once you have finalised the title of your book, I suggest you invest in a web address that aligns with its name.

Why is this important? Firstly, having a simple and memorable web address allows you to effortlessly promote your book to potential readers. Imagine being able to say, "You can pre-order my book at www.bookmarketingmadesimple.com" rather than directing them to a long and convoluted URL like 'www.librotas.com/your-book-title'. Not only does this enhance the professionalism of your author brand but it also makes it easier for people to find your book online.

It also enables you to create a centralised hub where interested readers can gather more information about your upcoming book. This webpage will serve as a powerful tool for promoting your book during the pre-selling phase, launch, and beyond.

Whilst purchasing the exact web address for your book is ideal, it may not always be available. In such cases, consider adding the word 'book' or '.book' to the title or explore other creative alternatives that align with your branding. If you already have multiple website domains, adding one more to the mix will be a breeze!

If you choose not to have a dedicated website, at the very least add a separate page solely dedicated to your book. This ensures that your book receives the attention and spotlight it deserves, allowing you to effectively promote it during this critical early stage.

Create compelling website copy

Creating compelling copy for your book's website or page is a vital step in enticing potential readers to pre-order your book. The words you choose have the power to captivate, persuade, and connect with your target audience. Although I talked about AIDA in chapter 3, here are some key tips that are specific to creating a really great pre-order page.

Start with an attention-grabbing headline: This will draw your readers in and persuade them to read on. You can go on to engage your readers by weaving a compelling narrative around your book. Share stories, anecdotes, or personal experiences that highlight the core themes and messages of your work. By tapping into the emotional aspects of storytelling, you can create a powerful connection with your audience, drawing them into the world you've created within your book.

Clearly communicate the unique selling points of your book: Identify what sets it apart from other similar titles in the market. Is it your fresh perspective, groundbreaking research, practical insights, or memorable methodology? Highlight these aspects in your copy to demonstrate the value your book brings to readers.

Understand the challenges, pain points, and aspirations of your target audience: Craft your copy in a way that directly addresses these concerns and positions your book as the solution they've been searching for. Show readers how your book will help them overcome obstacles, achieve their goals, or gain new knowledge and skills.

Use persuasive language: Use words and phrases that evoke emotion, create urgency, and inspire action. Tap into the power of descriptive language and strong calls to action to motivate readers to take the next step and pre-order your book.

Incorporate endorsements, testimonials, or reviews: You can build credibility and trust with social proof that adds validation to your book's value and can further convince potential readers to make the decision to pre-order.

Enhance the visual appeal of your book's website: Incorporate engaging graphics and imagery. If you already have your book cover design, you can feature a 2D or 3D mock-up on the page. This visual representation will help readers picture your book and create a sense of anticipation. Additionally, consider including a professional photograph of yourself to establish a personal connection with your audience.

Make it easy for potential buyers to pre-order your book: Consider integrating a popular payment gateway such as PayPal or Stripe that provides a user-friendly and trusted payment experience.

Strategically plan the timing of your pre-selling phase: Ideally, wait until you have a clear launch date in mind, such as when your book is in the editing and proofreading stages. This way, you can align your pre-selling efforts with the final stages of book preparation, giving you ample time to focus on marketing and generating pre-orders.

When promoting your book, be transparent with your audience about the expected distribution date: As you will be accepting pre-orders before you are ready to ship, you will need to manage your readers' expectations. In case of any unforeseen delays, promptly update your buyers and consider offering them exclusive previews or bonus content to thank them for their patience.

Refine your message: Remember, your website copy should convey the essence of your book, resonate with your target audience, and compel them to take action. You can refine your copy based on feedback, test different messaging approaches to find what resonates most effectively with your readers, and employ the methods that work for you. For example, instead of words, you could feature a video if that is preferred by you and your readers. A well-crafted website can be the key to capturing the attention and interest of your audience, leading to increased pre-orders and a successful book launch.

Offer incentives for pre-orders: Providing readers with an extra reason for them to commit early can increase their excitement and sense of exclusivity. Consider offering a special discounted price for pre-orders or including bonuses with limited availability. These bonuses could be in the form of an exclusive webinar, report, download, video, or audio recording that is only accessible to those who pre-order within a specific date period. Incentives not only reward early supporters but also create a sense of urgency, fostering a frenzy of anticipation before your book is even published.

Promote it far and wide: Utilise all the connections you've made to date; ask them to share it, buy it, and promote it so that you reach more people with your book. Actively tell people about your book on social media, through your mailing list and all of the other marketing channels you have decided to use to date.

Let me share examples from Sally Kay and Sheryl Andrews who took different approaches to pre-selling their books.

CLIENT STORY
Sally Kay
author of *Reflexology Lymph Drainage*

Sally's book, *Reflexology Lymph Drainage*, is a full colour 'coffee table' book for reflexologists who want to learn Sally's methodology for supporting those with breast cancer related lymphoedema and other inflammatory and auto-immune conditions.

Just before launching her book, Sally decided to add a page to her website to take pre-orders for her book. Containing well over 200 images, it's a beautifully illustrated guide, which is available for purchase for £49.99, so you may wonder how this would impact on the actual sales of her book.

When she launched it for pre-order she had a slightly discounted offer and within the first few weeks she had sold 325 copies which she personally signed, beautifully packaged, and lovingly posted. Without a desire to become an Amazon bestseller, she accidentally rocketed to the top of the charts when she sold 591 copies online during her launch period.

Although the income from book sales certainly wasn't Sally's motivation for writing her book, her altruistic vision is to reach more people and spread her message far and wide. But when you have a plan to do this, book sales are automatically going to follow. When I last heard from Sally in May 2023, she'd sold well over 3000 copies of her book.

CLIENT STORY
Sheryl Andrews
author of *Manage your Critic – From Overwhelm to Clarity in 7 Steps*

I introduced you to Sheryl earlier. Before she had a website to promote her book, Sheryl took an innovative way of promoting it. At her mastermind group she happened to mention that if she really thought people were waiting for the book it would motivate her to finish it. At this point two of the members literally threw her cash and said they wanted to read it. This prompted her to post on Facebook which resulted in 25 other people also wanting her book. She had so many people asking for her book that she had to keep a record on her whiteboard to remind her who had said they were interested. And every one of them bought a copy.

This was a great incentive for her to finish it, and a great incentive to create a page where people could easily buy it!

Key considerations when pre-selling your book

In the early days, you're likely to be distributing your book yourself, unless you outsource it to someone you trust. Once the books arrive, it is likely you'll have a production line going on where you'll be packaging up the books!

What I love about doing this myself is that in the past I've been able to add the wow factor with branded bookmarks, personalised mini chocolates and I've also signed the books, something that was still mentioned by my clients many years later. You could also add a postcard, letter, or special offer note for a product or programme if that's relevant to your book.

It's worth getting organised in advance. When you have a system in place to distribute your book, it will be easier. I have some brightly coloured jiffy envelopes, a standard letter in place, postage readily available, and labels ready to print the address when an order comes in, and a return address label to stick on the back of the envelope.

One of the main advantages of pre-selling your book is that, because you are distributing it yourself, you retain the profit after printing and distributing the book, though it's no substitute for using other platforms later on.

In addition, it's important to note that, after your launch, you can continue to use the website page you have created with a few tweaks. You might offer a signed copy through your website or have a special offer for someone who wants to buy directly from you.

Lastly, if you do decide to pre-sell your book, it's important to consider the timing and potential challenges of combining it with other promotional strategies like crowdfunding or an Amazon bestseller launch. Unless there is a significant time gap between them, your list and community might not appreciate multiple book promotions. However, if you have a reliable joint venture team in place for later stages, it may be worth exploring these options to boost your book's visibility and rise in the Amazon charts.

For an outline of some of the resources that I use and useful websites, please go to www.librotas.com/free for more information.

THINGS TO THINK ABOUT

Pre-selling your book is a great way to create frenzy and a buzz whilst you are finishing it. It will also give you some income to fund your book's publication and help prepare to market your book.

Take some time to create the compelling copy to promote your book on your website, whether you use words or decide to record a video.

Be realistic with your timescales as the final parts of publishing may take a little time — you have less control if other people are doing this stage for you.

Add an incentive for ordering your book early and post it out with a little something that gives it the wow factor.

Keep it simple; tell people about the book and add social proof in the form of reviews from people who have already read it.

_____

_____

_____

_____

_____

CHAPTER 12
Create a crowdfunding campaign

Crowdfunding has recently become a powerful tool for individuals and businesses to raise funds for their projects, causes, and creative endeavours. Authors, in particular, have recognised the potential of crowdfunding to not only finance their books but also to connect with a larger audience and build a supportive community. This chapter explores the concept of crowdfunding and its application in the world of publishing alongside a little used option of seeking sponsorship for your book's project.

When I was in the final stages of writing the first edition of this book, I considered crowdfunding it. The main reason being that I didn't feel that I could mention something in this book if I'd not done it myself. Since then, some of my friends and clients have taken this approach and their stories will be shared in this chapter.

At its core, crowdfunding involves raising funds via soliciting small contributions from a large number of people, typically through online platforms. Various crowdfunding platforms exist, some specifically tailored to cater to authors' needs. To assist you further, I have compiled a list of resources and links on www.librotas.com/free.

One significant advantage of crowdfunding is the potential to reach a wider audience and generate greater exposure for your book. However, it is crucial to note that failure to meet the funding target on certain platforms may result in being unable to proceed with your project. Nevertheless, the journey itself can elevate your profile and enable you to disseminate your message effectively.

Let me start by introducing you to Ellen Watts. When she published her first book, *Cosmic Ordering Made Easier*, she went down the crowdfunding route. Although she wasn't successful in meeting her crowdfunding goal, it did attract more clients and she learnt a lot from the process. Here are her top 14 tips.

 TOP 14 CROWDFUNDING TIPS BY ELLEN WATTS

1. Choose the platform that suits your needs: There are choices of crowdfunding platforms; some guarantee the money but those generally have a higher % fee; others only pay out if you reach your target, otherwise the deal's off. Personally, I chose the latter because I liked having the target and the 'all or nothing to play for' feel. I thought it was fair and also had the potential for excitement. After some research, I chose Kickstarter for my project and would choose them again.

2. Follow the instructions and the advice on the site: Complete the profile page in full, and include pictures and the story of why you wrote the book and who it will help. Use the expertise of your crowdfunding platform as they'll have run hundreds if not thousands of campaigns. They know what works and what doesn't.

3. Choose your time frame carefully: Shorter campaigns get more momentum, but give yourself enough time for the word to get around. I was impatient on my first one and chose three weeks, but I wasn't really ready to get promoting. A few distractions meant the campaign failed, and it didn't raise the funds I'd set as a target. Now I plan to set my target for around 12 weeks.

4. Make a video: It doesn't have to be fancy; just you talking is fine, but if you have a mock-up of the book or other props, so much the better. People need to connect with you as the author and hear your passion for your book.

5. Don't set your target too high: With crowdfunding, it's better to set a slightly lower goal than you'd really like and bust it sky high, than set a stretching one and miss it. So I suggest working out your real goal i.e. how much do you really need to be able to create your book and get it published, and then set your crowdfunder for the minimum you need to make that happen. Then set up another goal just for you which is twice as much and aim for that. Then, if you hit 50% of your secret goal, you will have had a successful campaign in your crowdfunders' eyes and will get paid the money, but chances are because your focus was higher, you will sail past the 50% with ease!

6. Don't expect the donations to come from friends: You don't want to feel you're nagging your mailing list or family and friends to death, although if your offer's good enough, you shouldn't need to. The sweetest surprise for me was how much traffic came from the Kickstarter community itself. There are people on there looking to help, plus get bargains and exclusive inclusions. Doing a crowdfunder is a great way of building your list if you're ready to take advantage.

7. Have a range of offers including ones that don't cost you much in time or effort: I included tiny ones like for £2 they could get 'a special report' which was not available anywhere else. I also had a £5 one 'My Top 20 Cosmic Ordering Tips' sent as an A4 PDF – PLUS a special thanks personal video message explaining the tips in a little more depth.

Having these small starter investments meant anyone could support me and feel they'd contributed even if they didn't have a lot of money. They don't have to be shipped – so all the funds raised are profit – and you only have to do the PDF or video once and it can be repurposed later.

Likewise, have a couple of very high end offers. These are likely to take up a good deal of your time – like a VIP day – so make only a few available and you don't need many to reach your total. Don't hold your breath expecting this to be taken up, but remember if it's not listed they can't pledge for it, and having it there gives your book some credibility. My top end package at £2400 or more was my 'Get it sorted apprenticeship'.

8. Showcase your book: In the middle of your offers will be your book itself and possibly your book plus book launch tickets. Again be mindful of numbers and how many you can cope with delivering, and put a maximum number rather than causing yourself a logistic and fulfilment crisis if things should take off wildly. PLUS scarcity often encourages people to take action immediately.

9. Be creative: What backers love most is 'can't buy in the shops' specials, so things like adding their name to a roll of honour in the book, if that's possible, will raise extra funds with little extra investment on your part.

10. Add up your offers: When all your offers are listed make sure that the total exceeds your target. This seems obvious, but I've seen some campaigns that haven't done this, and there's no way that they can hit their target even if they have sold everything that they have listed.

11. Campaign your campaign: Share it on social media, pop it in your newsletter and email your list, get networking, speaking, and mention it everywhere. Get some buzz up around reaching your target.

12. Update your pledgers regularly: Nurture these lovely new contacts and get them into your world as soon as you can via your list and social media.

13. Keep your promises: Broken promises are the number one cause of unhappy customers, so give priority to fulfilling orders soon after the campaign has finished.

14. Even if your campaign is not successful, it is not a failure: You will have attracted and made contact with people interested in your work and had some pledges that you can now follow up outside of the platform. For me, I see very little risk in attempting a campaign other than a little time and effort, but the potential to gain a great deal is very real.

Ellen Watts, www.ellen-unlimited.com, author of *Cosmic Ordering Made Easier: how to have more of what you want more often* and *Get it Sorted – for once, for all, for GOOD.*

I have two new stories to share with you. My good friend, Paul Newton, crowdfunded his book and I interviewed him in 2021 for my Smart Author System Community and Fast Track members, because he is a good example of someone who had great success before his book was published.

Paul Newton made the decision to write his book during the COVID-19 pandemic because, like many people, his business collapsed overnight. As a magician and mind reader, events and speaking gigs he had lined up were cancelled. Although the pandemic gave him time to write his book, he had no work and little money in the bank to plough into the production and marketing, and someone suggested that he crowdfunded his book by using the Crowdfunder platform.

He knew that it would have multiple benefits. People could pay for his book and get other money-can't-buy merchandise before his book was released, and he would have money to fund the project.

Paul had two targets: £2000 would allow him to scrape through and launch the book, and £4000 would enable him to launch the book in a way that he would be proud of. He managed to raise

£6885 – far more than he'd ever anticipated! His book *MentalTheft* was published in 2020.

What was Paul's secret? He had different levels of investment that people could make, from a £5 donation through to a £1500 corporate sponsorship option, and various packages in between. He gave himself a month to focus on the crowdfunder and used his networks and connections to help him succeed.

CLIENT STORY
Della Judd

author of *Get The Job You Really Want... In a Post-pandemic World*

Della was one of my Smart Author – Fast Track clients in 2021 and she attended one of the monthly masterclasses where I invited Paul Newton, as detailed above, to share his crowdfunding experience.

Della was inspired by Paul's story. So much so that she decided to crowdfund her book. She followed the 'buy one, donate one' crowdfunding approach, which enabled her to raise £3k before her book was published, a slightly different approach to getting the backing for her book.

Although she had an altruistic reason for doing the crowdfunder, it has also given her massive publicity, and many new supporters. She developed partnerships with organisations in Milton Keynes to help distribute the book and they supported her with the promotion and the launch.

As well as the successful funding campaign, it also led to 154 jobseekers in need getting a copy of her book for free. I interviewed Della later as a bonus for some of my Smart Author members to inspire them to use crowdfunding for their book!

Get sponsorship for your book

I know that crowdfunding isn't for everyone but if appeals to you then follow the advice from those who have already done it!

Before I move on, I'd like to share with you a slightly different but related approach. If crowdfunding isn't the right option for you, have you thought about seeking sponsorship for your book? Unlike crowdfunding where you will seek a larger number of individuals who will support your book, sponsorship relies on you approaching a small number of individuals or organisations to partner with you on the project and fund the process. I will leave you with Kate Barrett's story to explain how this could work.

CLIENT STORY
Kate Barrett
author of *E-telligence*

Kate's book is for corporate marketing teams who run email marketing campaigns, so we decided to explore sponsorship as a great way to self-fund her book.

As Kate already had valuable connections in the industry, she approached email providers and offered three levels of sponsorship. Sponsorship amounts ranged from £500–£2k with benefits commensurate with the fee involved, such as the inclusion of case studies in the book, a presence on her online platform, webinar with their clients, and 50–100 copies of her book.

She partnered with five organisations who sponsored the book, which not only covered her mentoring and publishing fees, it also enabled her to help them to reach more people with their products and expertise.

As a result of this approach, due to the exposure she got through the webinars she delivered for her partners, it helped her to reach thousands more people and sell almost 1000 copies of her book within the first six weeks.

THINGS TO THINK ABOUT

Crowdfunding works when you already have a good community in place and have support from others to raise the funds.

Be realistic with your target, as with many crowdfunding platforms you won't be successful unless you reach your target. There are a few platforms where you're still successful if you don't reach your target, but you will still need to deliver on your promise.

Have a range of different offers available from a small donation to a higher value item that could be one of your services, a product, or sponsorship of a programme or podcast.

Don't underestimate the time that it will take to crowdfund your book, but you will reap the rewards if your project is successful. You're more likely to achieve success if you have a great plan to achieve it, and are prepared to hustle to reach your target!

If you already work in an industry where you have great connections, you could consider seeking sponsorship for your project instead of crowdfunding or any other form of self-funding.

_____

_____

SECTION 2:
PREPARING TO LAUNCH YOUR BOOK

By now you will have poured your heart and soul into writing your book. Your manuscript will have been crafted and it is likely that you have entered the publishing process. It's now time to get ready for the actual launch!

Ideally, you'll start this phase a little before your launch (around two to three months earlier is ideal) to give you enough time to put the strategies into place so that your launch is a success.

Launching a book successfully is more than pressing the publishing button and sitting back and hoping the sales will start to roll in. It requires strategic actions and well-planned systems to ensure your book's success. That's where this section comes in.

In the following chapters, we will delve into the activities that will pave your path to a successful book launch. By implementing some or all of these strategies, you will not only captivate potential readers but also harness the momentum you've built during the pre-launch phase. The buzz surrounding your book will have already started to take shape, with eager readers waiting in anticipation, some even pre-ordering their copies.

There are four main areas that I will focus on at this stage:

Amplify your Amazon profile: I will guide you through the process of optimising your listing in the most popular online marketplaces (Amazon, bookstores, and other online distributors), ensuring it reaches the hands of eager readers worldwide.

Become a bestseller: I will show you how you can propel your book up the bestsellers list with an Amazon launch with the power of targeted marketing and strategic promotions to secure the coveted bestseller spot.

Power up your publicity: From media features to online promotions, I will explore the different ways to raise your book's visibility so you reach more new people with your book.

Build a buzz at your book launch: Discover how to throw a celebration party that not only commemorates your book's journey but also generates excitement and engages your audience in a memorable way.

These four elements, along with additional bonus tips, will be explored in the following five chapters. I will share practical strategies and insights you need to position your book and maximise your impact.

As you embark on the launch stage, it's natural to feel the urge to explore post-launch strategies simultaneously. While those strategies hold their own importance and I suggest you review them, you are probably more likely to factor them into your longer term marketing plan.

CHAPTER 13
Amplify your Amazon profile

It's crucial to ensure your book is available on platforms like Amazon, other online book outlets, and ideally physical bookshops worldwide. In this chapter, I will focus on the marketing collateral you need to successfully launch your book on Amazon. Whilst Amazon may be a love-it-or-hate-it platform, there's no denying its status as the go-to choice for authors looking to list their books.

Let me share some eye-opening statistics with you. According to New Digital Age, a staggering 86% of Brits shop on Amazon, with a quarter of the UK adult population subscribed to Amazon Prime[6]. Additionally, research by Feedvisor reveals that 66% of consumers initiate their product searches on Amazon, overshadowing the 20% who start on Google[7].

Clearly, Amazon's dominance in the online retail space is undeniable. However, rest assured that many of the tips I share here can also benefit you in getting your book noticed on other platforms that distribute and sell books.

I'm sure I don't need to tell you that simply listing your book on Amazon and waiting for sales to pour in isn't a good strategy. It requires fundamental groundwork to maximise your book's visibility. Fortunately, there are straightforward strategies you can employ to organically climb the bestseller ranks and attract your ideal readers on Amazon. What's more, several of these strategies can be seamlessly integrated with an Amazon launch, which I will delve into further in chapter 14 to boost your book sales.

By implementing these techniques, you can ensure your book gets attention, engages readers, and paves the way for its success in the highly competitive Amazon marketplace.

Choose the right book title

Choosing the right book title and subtitle for your book may be one of the most challenging aspects of writing a book. Whilst some authors find it easy, especially when it aligns directly with their programme or brand, some people struggle.

Let's take this book as an example. When I was originally writing the first edition in 2016, my working title was How to Market your Book on a Budget, but as I reviewed the final edits, I realised it didn't accurately represent the content. Some of the strategies I share require a significant investment, although they can yield substantial returns when executed effectively. Fortunately, a chance conversation with a friend and client helped me to nail the title. She helped me to home in on the book's promise: to simplify the process of marketing a book.

When selecting your book title, avoid being overly clever as you want to make it easily discoverable by people who are unfamiliar with you. I recommend incorporating words that resonate with your ideal reader in the title and/or subtitle. This ensures that your book's message and target audience are clear and will meet their expectations.

Have a well-designed book

They say people don't judge a book by its cover, but when it comes to actual books, I couldn't disagree more! Although you should consider this aspect earlier in the writing process, it's worth mentioning it here. The thumbnail of your book's front cover will be the first impression readers have on your Amazon listing, so it's crucial to ensure it looks professional and translates well into a small picture. Avoid overcrowding it with excessive information or using complicated images.

Your book cover doesn't have to be intricate or expensive. In fact, sometimes all you need is the right text to make it stand out! I delve deeper into the topic of creating a compelling cover in *Your Book is the Hook* (www.yourbookisthehook.com). It covers valuable insights including finding a good designer who can bring your ideas to life and create a cover that wows your readers.

However, the design of your book extends beyond its cover. The internal layout plays a crucial role in shaping your reader's experience. Factors like font size, white space, paragraph length, and the presence of subheadings significantly impact whether someone decides to purchase your book and read it until the end. So, pay attention to these details to ensure an enjoyable reading experience.

Ensure your book is professionally edited

Having a visually appealing listing for your book is essential, but it's equally important to ensure that your book's content is of high quality. Spelling and grammar mistakes, as well as poor flow, can hinder your book's success.

When readers download or receive a physical copy of your book, they expect a professional and polished reading experience that reflects your brand. To achieve this, it's crucial to invest in professional editing and proofreading services before publishing, even if you're on a budget.

Whilst I cover this topic extensively in my other books and programmes, I want to emphasise the significance of having a strong opening, especially when utilising the 'Look Inside' function. I will delve into this in more detail later in this chapter.

Remember, the professionalism of your book's content not only enhances its readability but also establishes credibility and trust with your readers.

Hone your book description

The back cover of your book and the blurb that you place on your website, Amazon, and other online stores play a significant role in your book's success.

Whilst writing the first edition of this book, I was contacted by someone who had published her book, but was struggling to get sales. Upon examining her Amazon page, I saw that she had only provided three lines of text in the book description area. One of the recommendations I made to her was to improve this section with compelling copy.

In your book description, you have the opportunity to provide a clear idea of what your book is about, and capture your reader's attention with a compelling hook. Particularly on Amazon, it is essential to organically incorporate keywords that will enhance your book's discoverability. If you review the information I shared in chapter 11, this will stand you in good stead in creating this text, as you may use similar information to your sales page.

Additionally, consider including endorsements and reviews from readers who have already enjoyed your book. This social proof can be influential in encouraging new readers to engage with your work and leave their own reviews on Amazon.

Price your book realistically

If you've not already set a price for your book, be realistic when making your decision. Most physical books in the non-fiction arena sell for somewhere in the region of £12.99–£19.99, and Kindle books typically have lower price points due to reduced production costs. Although you might argue that the same knowledge and expertise is involved with writing it, pricing psychology comes into play. There's a sweet spot where the price becomes a no-brainer for your ideal reader, prompting them to make a purchase without a second thought.

If you are self-publishing, bear in mind that selling your book on Amazon incurs costs. The cost of selling, printing and shipping your books will be taken from Amazon BEFORE you are paid your royalties, and it's not unusual to make only a few pounds from selling your book. This cost will vary dependent on number of pages, trim size, paper, and colour options.

This might cause you to wonder why you should distribute your book on Amazon, but trust me when I say that if you focus on the opportunities you are likely to generate off the back of your book, then it is worth it.

It may be worth accepting a small or no profit on the book itself if it generates additional income for your business through related services or products. It really is a strategic decision that involves balancing the perceived value of your book against the market expectations and the financial goals you have for your business.

And remember you can sell your book directly alongside this, for example, to individuals at networking events, speaking engagements, or exhibiting.

Choose the right categories and keywords

Now that you have all the necessary information to list your book, let's explore a few additional strategies to optimise your profile.

Selecting the right categories for your book is crucial in helping your ideal readers find you. If you're unsure what categories to choose, a helpful approach is to examine competing books with high sales and see which categories they are listed under. This can provide valuable insights to inform your decision.

To delve deeper into category and keyword research, a useful tool you may consider investing in is Publisher Rocket, a software tool designed to assist authors and publishers with their book marketing efforts. It offers features such as book keyword research, Amazon KDP category research, Amazon Ads optimisation, and competitor analysis.

One of the key features of Publisher Rocket is its ability to generate a list of relevant keywords for your book by analysing Amazon search data. Additionally, it can aid in Amazon advertising by identifying profitable keywords and categories to target in your advertising campaigns.

Keywords play a vital role in helping your book get discovered, similar to how SEO-friendly keywords are essential for website visibility. To identify relevant keywords for your book on Amazon, you can start by typing search terms and observing the suggested ideas that pop up. Another approach is to use the Google Keyword Planner tool, which I mentioned earlier in the book. Alternatively, AI tools like ChatGPT can also assist in refining keywords for your book.

Let me share Nick Fewings' experience of using Publisher Rocket.

CLIENT STORY
Nick Fewings
author of *Team Lead Succeed*

When Nick realised that Amazon had not assigned his book to the relevant categories when first published, he used Publisher Rocket to update the categories it was in, and also to change the keywords.

This has worked well, as in the Professional Development Category it has ranked in the Top 30 at some point during each month since he amended the categories.

Publisher Rocket also enabled him to choose categories that, whilst relevant, did not have as much competition. In May 2023, he decided to make the Kindle version free for two days, as it coincided with Paying It Forward day, to see if it could get to the number one spot on Amazon, which it successfully achieved under the category of Business Management and Leadership on Kindle.

Develop your Amazon author page

Did you know that you can have an Amazon author profile? If you've already got your book listed and you don't yet have a profile, do it now through the Author Central section on Amazon. This platform provides you with the opportunity to showcase yourself as an author, link to your books, share your biography to help readers get to know you better, and include additional elements such as photos, videos, and more. The best part is that it's completely free!

Having an Amazon author page allows readers to click on your name in your book listing and find out more about you. They can discover other books you have published and get a deeper understanding of your work.

Additionally, your Amazon author page provides a convenient way for you to view your books, sales rankings, and reviews all in one place, so you can monitor your book's performance on the platform.

Use the Look Inside function

The Look Inside feature (also known as Search Inside) allows customers to preview the content of a book before making a purchase. It provides an online preview of the book's contents, including the cover, table of contents, initial pages, and selected pages from the middle of the book. This feature is displayed on your book's product page on Amazon.

Enabling this function gives potential readers the opportunity to browse through your book, sample its contents, and determine if it's the right book for them before purchasing it.

It's worth noting that the Look Inside feature plays a role in Amazon's search algorithm. When a prospective reader searches for a specific keyword or phrase that appears in the preview of a book, it may assign a higher ranking to that book in the search results.

Have an e-book and a physical book

This leads me to my next point. I am often asked whether you need to have a physical print book and an e-book. I believe that there is a market for both formats for several reasons.

Offering both options give your readers the freedom to choose their preferred reading experience. If you want to make a Kindle (e-book) version of your book available, you will need to sign up to KDP (Kindle Direct Publishing).

Having an e-book allows readers to download a sample and get a taste of your book's content. Similar to using the 'Look Inside' function, it helps readers assess if your book resonates with them. Additionally, I recommend distributing your e-book on platforms beyond Amazon to reach a wider audience.

Also, if you are writing a book to build your authority, having a physical book is essential, especially if you plan to speak, run training sessions, or participate in physical events where you showcase your expertise. You can't do a book signing without a physical book!

You may wish to have an audiobook as well, and I will talk more about digital and audiobooks in chapter 18.

Get lots of excellent Amazon reviews

Once your book is published, I recommend you actively seek reviews for your book, as books with a higher number of positive reviews tend to be more popular among readers, which is an important factor in Amazon's ranking algorithm. They also indicate that the book is well received and engaging. It may then appear in the 'Customers who bought this item also bought' section when people are searching for similar books.

Reviews also contribute to the relevancy of a book in Amazon's search results. When a book has numerous reviews that mention keywords or phrases, the algorithm may consider it more relevant.

Reviews serve as social proof for potential buyers, demonstrating that other people have read and enjoyed the book. Positive reviews can increase the likelihood that a potential buyer will purchase the book, which can lead to more sales and higher rankings. However, it's worth noting that not all reviews are weighted equally.

Amazon gives more importance to verified reviews (reviews written by those who have purchased the book on Amazon) than unverified reviews. Additionally, factors such as recency and helpfulness of reviews can influence a book's ranking.

It's important to remember that receiving reviews lower than five stars is normal, as every reader has their own opinion of a book. You can choose to consider the feedback and explore opportunities for improvement. If you come across a review that is malicious or misleading, you can report it to Amazon and request its removal. However, genuine reviews that express genuine opinions are generally not removed.

Please note that it's always a good idea to follow Amazon's guidelines and policies regarding reviews and their solicitation to ensure compliance and maintain a positive reputation as an author.

Be a reseller for your books

In many cases, publishers will automatically include your book for distribution on Amazon. However, if your publisher doesn't offer this, you can use Amazon Advantage to sell your books directly.

This allows you to have control over the distribution and availability of your book on Amazon.

Additionally, being a reseller for your book means that if Amazon runs out of copies or experiences a shortage, you can step in and fulfil those orders yourself. And, as a reseller, you have the flexibility to offer discounts and promotions for your book. This can attract potential buyers and encourage sales.

Keep in mind that managing your own inventory and fulfilling orders as a reseller requires additional effort and logistical considerations. However, it can provide you with more control over the availability and pricing of your book on Amazon.

Publish more than one book!

Many successful authors don't stop at just one book; they continue to publish multiple books over time, and this has various advantages on Amazon specifically. Firstly, when readers enjoy one of your books, they are more likely to seek out your other books, and they are likely to become fans of your writing and tell other people about you.

Secondly, multiple books allow you to diversify your offerings and cater to different readers. Each book can target a specific niche or explore different topics within your area of expertise, attracting a wider range of readers. Each book becomes an additional asset in your publishing portfolio and provides more opportunities for sales and income streams. Thirdly, via Amazon KDP you can link your books as a series of books if this is relevant.

Tell people your book is for sale

It may seem obvious, but it's crucial to actively promote and inform people about your book's availability for sale. If you list your book without telling people about it, your book will go unnoticed, resulting in low sales and limited business success. I have encountered numerous individuals who have faced this exact situation, which is one of the reasons why I've written this book.

Lastly, whilst Amazon is a popular platform, there are also other online bookstores and platforms where you can list and promote your book. Each platform has its own unique audience and reach, so by diversifying your distribution, you increase the likelihood of reaching a broader readership. Additionally, don't limit yourself to online platforms alone. I will explore further options later where you can sell physical copies of your book and connect directly with potential readers.

THINGS TO THINK ABOUT

There are many strategies you can take to enhance your Amazon profile before and once your book has been listed. Go through the list and implement them one by one as they all complement each other.

Social proof in the form of Amazon reviews will help your book's ranking, and don't worry if you get a poor review; at least it shows that the reviewer is real!

Like any form of marketing, keeping your Amazon profile and books up to date will enhance your book, even after it's been published.

Become a reseller for your book, even if your publisher also distributes your book, as this will allow people to buy your book directly.

Remember that Amazon isn't the only platform available so consider how you can use other online retailers to maximise the reach of your book.

_____

_____

_____

_____

_____

CHAPTER 14
Become a bestseller

When it comes to achieving success with your book, have you considered aiming for the sought-after status of becoming a bestselling author?

The Amazon number one bestseller ranking is a goal that many authors strive for, and with good reason. While it may not hold the same kudos it once did, reaching this milestone can still have a significant impact on your profile, visibility, and book sales. In this chapter, I will delve into the strategies and steps you can take to increase your chances of becoming a bestseller.

It's important to recognise that the pre-launch phase plays a crucial role in the overall success of your book launch. An effective Amazon bestseller campaign relies on you having built a strong community and collaborating with partners who will support you. Although you might also strive to become a bestseller on other lists such as *The New York Times* bestseller list, this requires a more substantial approach than I am sharing in this chapter.

Whilst the primary objective of an Amazon book launch is to secure the number one position in the Amazon charts, a well-executed bestseller campaign offers additional benefits to your book and your business. By reaching a broader audience, your book and personal brand gain increased visibility and have a better chance of being noticed.

There are various ways to hold an Amazon launch, from the simple to the complex. The following steps outline a straightforward version of the strategy that I have adapted from the insights and experiences shared by others in the field.

I personally applied this strategy successfully, propelling my first and second books to the number one spot on Amazon. It also proved effective when promoting my third book as a Kindle edition. Additionally, I successfully implemented it during the initial release of this book, and I thoroughly documented the process I used, which is now available as the 'Book Launch Blueprint' on my website, which I follow with some of my clients (you can find out more at www.librotas.com/booklaunchblueprint). I will share some examples from this launch throughout this chapter.

Here are the seven essential steps you need to take to launch your book on Amazon:

1. Decide your launch date
2. Create an offer
3. Ask other people to help you
4. Get ready for your launch
5. Help your helpers
6. Promote it yourself
7. Measure your success and follow up

Step 1: Decide your launch date

To maximise the effectiveness of your Amazon bestseller campaign, it's crucial to choose a specific launch date when a significant number of people can purchase your book within a short timeframe. Whilst selecting a weekday is generally advisable, consider your target audience and their online activity patterns.

To ensure a successful launch, allocate ample time for preparation. This includes creating assets and materials that will assist others in promoting your book, as well as securing the assistance of influential individuals who can help spread the word. Keep in mind that these influential partners often plan their marketing activities in advance, so allowing enough lead time is essential for their participation.

Step 2: Create an offer

To incentivise as many people as possible to buy your book on your launch day, I suggest you create an offer solely for that day. The simple version of this process is typically a discounted price for your book, such as 99p or 99 cents.

Alternatively, you could make it a little more complex and offer specific bonuses only valid on this date. These bonuses should complement your book and may include elements such as a training session, masterclass, complimentary access to a valuable training programme, or another product that supports your launch. It's important to note that these bonuses should be easy to deliver and not require too much of your time.

When I followed this process for the first edition of this book, I included interviews with two of my book experts, a book marketing checklist, and a Q&A webinar following the launch which also shared some of the strategies I followed to reach the Amazon bestseller spot.

If you want to add even more value and complexity to your offer, you can consider collaborating with other business owners who can provide their products or services as part of the offer. I did this for my first launch for *The Secrets of Successful Coaches*; however, be cautious as this can make the offer difficult to manage! Additionally, it may divert attention away from you as the focal point of the launch.

Step 3: Ask other people to help you

A crucial element of a successful Amazon launch is enlisting the support of others to expand your reach on your launch day. Ideally, you should aim for a long list of helpers, comprising individuals with a strong community of potential readers who align with your book's target audience.

When I wrote my first book, where I interviewed many coaches, I found that most of them were willing to share the information with their respective audiences and promote it on social media. This played a significant role in the success of my book promotion.

The most effective approach to engage your helpers is by creating a personalised email and sending it to each of them individually. This email should outline your book launch plan, provide a brief synopsis of your book, specify the launch date, and include a clear request for their assistance. Additionally, you can share the launch details on social media and invite people to apply to support your launch via an online form. I did both of these for the original launch of this book and by the time I reached my launch date I had around 100 supporting the launch.

Step 4: Get ready for your launch

If you are planning a more complex launch with bonuses or additional offers, it is essential to prepare a dedicated one-page webpage specifically for your launch. This page will provide details about your book, emphasise why people need to buy it, and showcase any supporting offers. This is the page you will direct people to on your launch day.

You need to ensure your page includes a prominent link to your Amazon page, making it easy for visitors to make a purchase alongside a sign-up link so people can register for bonuses. Ideally incorporate a sign-up box where your new reader can leave their name, email address, and Amazon order number. This enables them to also join your mailing list, which facilitates future follow-ups. Also, set up a thank you page and autoresponder emails to deliver any promised bonuses.

Step 5: Help your helpers

Once you have secured the support of your helpers for your book launch, provide them with the necessary tools and resources to promote your book effectively. Here's how you can assist your helpers:

Create promotional materials: Design emails, social media updates, and other promotional materials for your helpers to use. These materials should contain the key information you want them to share with their communities. It's important to give your helpers the option to customise these materials to suit their audience's preferences, especially in the case of standard emails.

Direct them to the launch webpage: Instruct your helpers to direct their followers to the dedicated launch webpage mentioned earlier or the link to your book if you have not created a specific page.

Send reminders: Prior to the launch day and on the day itself, send a friendly reminder to your helpers to keep them informed and engaged. Remind them of the launch date, the importance of their support, and express your gratitude for their willingness to help.

Thank your helpers: After the launch, make sure to thank your helpers for their assistance and support. Acknowledge their contribution and express your appreciation for their efforts.

Gratitude goes a long way in maintaining strong relationships and encouraging future collaborations.

Step 6: Promote it yourself

In addition to relying on your helpers, it is crucial that you take an active role in promoting your book yourself. Here are some strategies to consider:

Use your existing platforms: Leverage your newsletter, social media accounts, and any other platforms you have to promote your book. Craft engaging and compelling messages that highlight the value and benefits of your book and encourage your audience to make a purchase. The messages are likely to be variations of the information you have created for your helpers.

Explore different channels: Look for additional opportunities to promote your book beyond your usual platforms. This could include participating in relevant forums, engaging with communities in your niche, and actively participating in LinkedIn groups. Identify channels where your target audience congregates and tailor your messaging accordingly.

Consider paid advertising: Consider running targeted Facebook or Google advertisements to reach a wider audience. Develop ad campaigns that effectively communicate the value of your book and drive potential readers to your launch webpage or Amazon page.

Engage in conversations: Actively engage in relevant online conversations, such as forums or social media groups, where discussions about topics related to your book are taking place. Share valuable insights, answer questions, and subtly promote your book when appropriate. Additionally, consider attending physical events or networking opportunities where you can talk about your book and generate interest.

By promoting your book through various channels and adopting a multi-pronged approach, you increase its visibility and attract potential readers from different sources. Remember to start promoting early on the launch day to build momentum, maintain a consistent presence throughout the day, and keep the day free should you need to address any issues.

Step 7: Measure your success and follow up

Throughout your launch day, you can closely monitor your progress. Taking screenshots of your Amazon rankings throughout the day will enable you to compare your performance at different times and track your success. After the launch day, you can assess the outcome of your launch by analysing your launch results, sales data, ranking improvements, and reader feedback, which helps to determine whether your objectives have been met.

Through your mailing software, follow up with new readers who have purchased your book. As well as delivering the promised bonuses, you can provide additional value to your readers and also remind them to leave an Amazon review, as reviews are essential for social proof and attracting more readers.

It's important to note that while this launch plan is effective for getting your book noticed and achieving Amazon bestseller status, it is not a long-term strategy to maintain top rankings or secure other bestseller lists. To achieve sustained success, a comprehensive marketing plan must complement the launch process.

Remember that the primary goal of this launch is to reach a larger audience and connect with individuals who may not have otherwise discovered your work. By leveraging the Amazon bestseller status in your publicity, you can enhance your credibility and attract more readers to your book.

To wrap up this chapter, let me share some of the successes I had in 2017 when I launched the first edition of *Book Marketing Made Simple* by following this process.

By the time I reached the launch date, I had around 100 helpers agree to support the launch at some level, from those who simply supported my Thunderclap campaign (a tool that unfortunately is no longer in existence that supported a social media blast of the book promotion) to those who were willing to interview me or send an email to their list.

Thunderclap: I had 110 people sign up for the Thunderclap campaign with a social reach of 200,445 people.

Podcast and webinar interviews: I did seven interviews via podcast or video recording.

Magazine articles or guest blogs: I wrote five magazine articles or guest blogs that coincided with the launch and three people reviewed the book on their blogs.

Number of book reviews on Amazon: 26 people had left a five-star review on Amazon within 24 hours of the launch.

And yes, the book did reach the number one bestseller spot on Amazon!

 **THINGS TO THINK ABOUT**

The Amazon bestseller plan is just part of your launch strategy, and it is a great way to create a buzz with your book and reach more people.

It works best when you designate a specific launch date when you promote your book.

You'll achieve the greatest success when you get helpers on board in complementary fields who will help you with your promotion.

You need to help your helpers by giving them emails and social media updates that they can share with their audience. And make sure you share it with your own community – a lot!

Test and measure your success. Even if you don't reach the Amazon number one bestseller spot, hundreds, if not thousands, of new people will be aware of your book.

_____

_____

_____

_____

_____

CHAPTER 15
Power up your publicity

Your book has the potential to change lives and make a huge impact on the world, and it's only natural that you will want your message to reach a wider audience beyond your own community and partnerships. That's where this chapter comes in. Actively seeking publicity and getting media exposure for your book enables you to connect with new audiences and captivate your target audience, even before your book reaches their hands.

And the good news is that publicity is not limited to the launch stage of your book or confined to a single moment in time – you can seek publicity and media exposure for your book at any time, and actually it's not something you should forget about after your book is launched. At any stage, you might be approached to curate an article for your local newspaper, a national magazine, or you may get approached for a radio or television interview.

Whilst I was writing *The Mouse That Roars*, I secured an interview with a freelance journalist who wrote for the *Daily Express*. Even though the interview took place 18 months before the book was published, it was still a great coup for my business. Not only did I get a double page spread in the paper, but I had a photoshoot specifically for the piece – including makeup, hair, and photographer! I found out about the opportunity through a PR friend telling me about a #journorequest post on Twitter, and when contacted, the journalist was interested in the main story that I share in the book.

Between book publications in 2020, I was approached by a journalist for a piece in the *Daily Mail* Femail section, and some friends and I went to their offices in London for an all-day photoshoot.

I've had multiple articles published in physical and print publications over the years, and not all related to my business and my book. If an opportunity lands in my lap that feels relevant to how I can help and inspire people, I will usually say yes!

If you haven't yet explored the possibility of publicity to promote your new book, consider the potential it holds. Securing coverage in press outlets, magazines, radio programmes, or online publications can significantly expand your reach and introduce you to new audiences.

One thing that I would suggest you consider is having a dedicated media page on your website, especially after you have had a few publicity pieces under your belt. This page serves as a powerful tool to showcase your media features, providing a comprehensive overview of where you've been featured and allowing prospective interviewees to gain insight into your previous articles, podcasts, and interviews. You can include links to online articles, so people can easily click through and view the piece. Also include the details of how an interested journalist can contact you or one of your team.

In the past, I had a physical scrapbook, carefully preserving articles that highlighted my expertise and accomplishments. It included pieces I wrote for magazines, features where I was recognised as an expert, top tip articles, and much more. And now I have a media page on my website. By having this readily accessible resource, I can easily share my media presence with others and highlight the breadth and depth of my experience.

Now, let's delve into a couple of inspiring client stories, the first of which illustrates the transformative impact of publicity alongside other complementary approaches.

CLIENT STORY
Nick Fewings
author of *Team Lead Succeed*

When Nick Fewings published his first book in March 2022, one of his goals was to get publicity off the back of his book. Here are some examples of his success, which show his integrated approach.

Nick had an article featured in the *Edge Journal*, the magazine of the Institute of Leadership & Management. He had a review of his book in *Project*, the quarterly journal of the Association for Project Management (33,000 readership). It was undertaken by Richard Noble OBE, who held the land-speed record in Thrust2. In addition, he also had an article featured in April 2023 in the magazine, about efficiency and effectiveness, which mentions his book.

At the time of sharing his successes with me, Nick had completed two podcast interviews with two more in the pipeline. Plus, four webinars for the Association for Project Management and Project Management Institute (these are the biggest project management professional bodies in the UK and US respectively).

One of Nick's goals was to use his book to reach the US market and he has also had two articles published in the US for CAI, a global technology services provider.

Whilst he can't be specific on outcomes, he did notice a spike in bestseller ranking on Amazon both in the UK and US after each of the webinars he had undertaken.

CLIENT STORY
Lorraine Palmer
author of *Raw Food in a Flash*

As I alluded to earlier with my own experiences, here is another great example of someone who didn't wait until her book was published before she got publicity. Before her book was available, Lorraine was featured in three magazines: *Chat Magazine*, *The Funky Raw Magazine*, and *Wolverhampton Magazine*, where she was on the cover.

She was also approached by a newspaper wanting to feature an article on her story, and has done two podcasts and one live interview to date. As Lorraine went through the menopause prematurely, this was the hook that interested the journalists.

She also finds that people notice her more and doors are instantly open because they know that she has something important to say.

Create a press release

When it comes to promoting your non-fiction book, you may consider creating a well-crafted press release. It serves as a launch pad to generate interest and media coverage, allowing you to share your story and the transformative value of your work with the world. While a press release alone may not guarantee immediate publicity, it lays the foundation for captivating journalists and piquing their curiosity.

Achieving success with your press release involves more than simply sending it out blindly to a handful of journalists. The most favourable outcomes arise from building personal relationships with journalists who resonate with your target audience and who you have connected with on a deeper level.

It's important to note that journalists are not solely interested in your book itself, but rather the unique story behind it – the inspiration, experiences, or expertise that led you to write your book.

Using the services of a professional PR expert is worth considering. This allows you to focus on your strengths while the PR expert leverages their expertise to identify unique angles and stories that journalists will find captivating. They possess a network of valuable contacts and relationships with the right publications for your audience. It's worth noting that many journalists freelance for various publications, increasing the opportunities for exposure.

If you choose to handle your PR efforts independently, it's crucial to research the publications that your ideal readers engage with and make direct contact with editors and journalists who write articles relevant to your book's themes. If you haven't already compiled a media contact list, now is the perfect time to create one.

In addition to traditional media outlets, consider exploring opportunities with online publications, as they have become powerful platforms to reach and engage with your target audience. Many magazines feature dedicated book review sections, and there are book bloggers specialising in various areas of expertise who may be willing to review your book on their websites.

Keep your eyes open for potential opportunities as they may unexpectedly present themselves. One of my former clients saw a feature on BBC Breakfast and took to Facebook, asking her friends if anyone could connect her with the journalist involved. Thanks to her network, one of the presenters reached out to her personally, and through my PR contacts, she was guided to the right person at the BBC.

Remember, being proactive and willing to comment on current affairs can also yield fruitful results. One of my clients approached her local newspaper with an article on stress management just before National Stress Awareness Day, and they published her piece. If your book has a specific connection to a particular time of year or occasion, seize the opportunity to leverage it effectively.

Get radio and television interviews

Being interviewed on television or radio offers a tremendous opportunity to showcase your expertise and knowledge to a wide audience. I've had the privilege of experiencing both mediums, including a regular slot on a local radio station in the past.

Let me share a few examples of clients who have successfully leveraged radio and television interviews. Cath Lloyd had the honour of being featured on BBC Women's Hour in 2019, whilst Zoe Dronfield is frequently sought after for her insights on radio and TV discussions centred around the topic of domestic abuse, which she covers in her book. It's quite common for my clients to secure appearances on local radio stations, allowing them to connect with their immediate communities and beyond.

Now, I understand that the prospect of giving an interview may feel intimidating for some. That's why I reached out to my trusted publicist, Helen McCusker, to share her invaluable tips on mastering your first live radio interview. These insights were originally published in *Self Publishing Magazine* and are designed to help you navigate the experience confidently.

HOW TO GIVE YOUR FIRST RADIO INTERVIEW BY HELEN MCCUSKER

Helen McCusker is not only a book publicist but trained as a radio journalist and used to produce and present on many radio stations across the south coast of England. Here she shares her tips for on-air success when the time comes for you to give your first live interview.

So you're a new author, your book has been published and a radio producer has shown an interest in your story and has asked you to visit their studio to take part in a live interview. If you're like the majority of the authors I work with, you'll be feeling apprehensive and probably a little overwhelmed by the thought of being heard by thousands of listeners.

My background is in radio presentation and news; yes, that's right, I used to spend my working day in front of a microphone... and I used to love it! Radio is fun, and the best part is that you don't see any of those thousands that are tuned in listening to you and they can't see you either (unless of course there's a sneaky studio webcam!). So the best advice I can give you is to treat the interview as a casual one-to-one chat with a friend. You'll enjoy the experience and learn a lot from it for future media engagements.

Preparing yourself

As soon as the interview has been confirmed, post a review copy of your book to the producer with a press release and author biography to ensure the presenter has time to look over it before interviewing you. Note that I say 'look over it' – don't expect the presenter to have read it from cover to cover, because they usually won't have had time to.

It's also worth making it clear at this stage what you do (and what you don't) feel comfortable talking about, just to save any awkward silences on-air.

Tune in to the radio station and programme that you'll be interviewed on before your interview day to get a feel for the presenter's interviewing style and the target audience you'll be speaking to. You could ask the producer for information on the demographic and some potential questions that you might get asked.

Write down and practise key messages in a series of bullet points; this includes the title of your book, any supporting websites and your author name too (it's amazing what you can nervously forget whilst on-air, trust me!). Be able to explain what your book is about in a few sentences; many authors cannot do this, so give it a go before the big day arrives.

The day before your interview, confirm the date, time, place, and anticipated length of the interview with the producer in charge, just in case there have been any last minute changes to the schedule. Ensure you have their direct telephone number and that they have yours in case of emergency.

Be sure to let your social networks know that you'll be on-air so that they can tune in and offer you feedback; it's also another good excuse to let everyone know that you've published a book!

Arriving at the studio

On the day of the interview, allow plenty of time for the unexpected (traffic, parking space, bad weather, etc.). Most programmes will require you to arrive around 20 minutes before you are due to go on-air, to give you enough time to meet the producer, run through any concerns and grab a coffee or snack (remember to eat beforehand, otherwise a rumbling stomach could prove embarrassing when your microphone goes live!).

Be ready to meet other interesting people in the green room, the room where guests wait before they enter the studio. So take your business cards and do some all-important networking. When your time slot arrives, remember to switch your mobile phone off before you enter the studio and remove anything else from your person that might be distracting for you or the presenter (for example, noisy jewellery!). A glass of water is always useful to keep at hand just in case you have a tickly throat or cough during the interview, so ask the producer if they can organise one for you.

The interview

The most important thing is to relax and be yourself. Remember, you're the expert on your book and you've already proved that what you have to say is interesting, because you've been booked for a radio interview. Sit up straight, listen, talk slowly, and smile! It might sound silly, but listeners can sense your emotion from your voice and if you're not talking enthusiastically about your own book they may stop listening.

Of course, your story may be emotional in other ways and, if the subject matter is sensitive, you will need to adjust your interview style accordingly. Have a bullet point list in front of you so you have a clear idea of the direction the interview will take and the most important items you wish to discuss. Your interview will fly by and you don't want to go home with regrets, saying "I wish I'd talked about that!"

The trick is to covertly refer to your book wherever possible; you don't want the interview to sound like one big advertisement, but you can discreetly refer to it when answering questions – a 'soft sell' as such. For example, "In my book, The Author, I provide ten tips for writing a book. We don't have time to talk about all of these right now, but let me read you the first two..."

If your book is business related in any way then be careful of using confusing jargon, as you need to get your message across clearly and in a relatively short space of time. If quoting statistics, have a summary of the facts in your notes, so you can easily and accurately quote them. Keep your answers brief and to the point as there is nothing worse than a rambling author who doesn't let the presenter guide the interview. In radio, the term 'sound bite' refers to good, informative, snappy answers which convey a point clearly and succinctly.

Towards the end of the interview, have your contact details in front of you to read out: website, Facebook, Twitter addresses, and of course, those all-important book details such as price and local stockists.

Follow-up

Radio programmes can usually be accessed online for a short time after broadcast, so why not have a listen back and analyse your interview strengths and weaknesses? Be warned, it can take some time to get used to the sound of your own voice!

Record a copy of the interview and ask the radio station if you can upload it to your website, which they will usually be fine with, as long as you post a full credit alongside. Most radio programmes these days have Facebook and Twitter pages, so ask the producer if a link to your website or Amazon page can be uploaded for listeners to find out more about you and your book.

Finally, send the producer and presenter an email to say thank you, and volunteer yourself for future interviews. It's always worth asking for their feedback too as we all have areas we can improve on and this will prepare you even more for interview number two. Good luck and most of all, enjoy!

Helen McCusker is a freelance book publicist who helps authors to achieve high profile media coverage and boost their book sales. You can connect with Helen via Twitter: @helenmccusker or Instagram: @book_publicist

Be proactive

You can probably see that there are many ways that you can get publicity for your book, and the places you wish to be featured will depend on your ideal audience. As with any of the marketing techniques, be proactive, have a plan, and make sure you follow up with those people whom you've contacted.

Do bear in mind that although local publications may ask for a quote or an article and publish it immediately to fill a space in their publication, and you may be asked for your opinion on a breaking news article, there is a long lead time for some publications. Glossy magazines will be thinking around 4–6 months ahead, so if you are being proactive rather than reactive with your publicity campaign, do bear this in mind. And if publicity is a core part of your launch, do get an expert to help you.

You may have to react to a media opportunity quickly. The trick with being ready for any such opportunity is to know your content well. It's amazing how quickly you may forget the content of your book after you've written it! Have a range of different ways you can share your expertise, as you may find yourself put on the spot, especially if you're live on the radio or TV.

 **THINGS TO THINK ABOUT**

Remember that journalists are not interested in your book, but they are interested in stories, whether they are yours or your clients'.

Have a bank of article topics that you can share with magazines and newspapers that will interest them and their readers. Consider notable days when your local press or radio may be interested in your content.

If time is your biggest barrier to seeking publicity and this is a core part of your launch, then make sure you seek the assistance of an expert who can use their already established contacts to support your launch.

Be prepared to be interviewed at the drop of a hat, as once you're noticed, you'll be approached by journalists as an expert in your field, and you may well be asked for your comment on topical stories.

Always look for opportunities for publicity, whether it's a book review or a feature in an online magazine.

_____

_____

_____

_____

CHAPTER 16
Build a buzz at your book launch

A great way to create a buzz when your book is released is to hold a book launch party for your book. When your months of hard work – if not longer – come to fruition, this is a pivotal moment to not only celebrate your own work, but also thank those people who are close to you. I'm sure they've been your greatest champions and have had to put up with you during this period!

As an author, holding a book launch party is also a powerful way to raise the profile of your book and bring together your clients and supporters. I have personally experienced the immense benefits of these events, with each book launch paving the way for new connections, clients, and opportunities that have propelled my business forward.

In this chapter, I will delve into the art of hosting a book launch party, exploring various approaches and strategies. Whether you prefer a simple yet intimate signing in a local bookstore or an elaborate affair in a luxury hotel, the possibilities are endless. Additionally, I will explore the exciting arena of online launches, which can complement or even replace traditional in-person events.

My experiences

In my opinion, having a party is a great way of launching your book. There are various ways of doing this and it's important to consider your plan of action from the very beginning. Let me share my own experiences as I've held four very different book launches to date.

The launch for my first book, *The Secrets of Successful Coaches*, took place at a beautiful hotel in Hampshire in a room overlooking the sea, where over 70 people joined the celebration. A free event, it included tea, coffee, and cupcakes branded with my business logo. As part of the event, we incorporated a charity element through a book raffle where other authors kindly donated copies of their books. After an initial period of networking, my mentor and two of my business friends gave talks, and I then had the chance to tell people about the book. I had a professional photographer (which gave me publicity photos that continue to serve me today), and after the speeches and raffle I did a book signing.

The second book launch, for *How to Stand Out in your Business*, was part of a multi-speaker event – the Star Biz conference – that I ran in 2012. The spotlight veered away from my new book, being somewhat overshadowed by my excellent speakers, magician, and our firewalk experience! I did have a videographer and photographer for this event, providing me with valuable material afterwards.

My third and fourth book launches were similar in their approach, and, for both, I charged a small fee that included a signed copy of my book. My third book launch was for *Your Book is the Hook*, and for this event I had a branded cake that was designed to look like the book cover. Although this wasn't cheap, it was a great bit of PR! For this launch, graphic recording expert Emma Paxton graphically recorded the event by illustrating it as it happened on a big sheet of paper. As she'd already provided the illustrations for the book, it brought the two things together. It was a great talking point on the day and provided me with a souvenir of the event.

My fourth book launch, for *The Mouse That Roars*, centred around my personal story, and was held in a beautiful cosy local café. We created a goody bag for this event and had a scrumptious vegan buffet and cake. Attendees also had the chance to win a book hamper, which was a great PR opportunity for my author friends who donated a copy of their book for the event. Notably, this launch was videoed, giving me useful footage to promote the book and the launch for many months after the event.

When I launched the first edition of this book, I opted for an Amazon launch rather than a physical launch (which I explored in chapter 14). Each of the launches has been memorable and I will share some more client stories later so you can see the approach they have taken.

The purpose of your book launch

Before I get into the logistics of what to include and how to do it, I'd like you to consider the purpose of your book launch and what you want to get from it.

- Is it to thank your clients, family, and friends?
- Is it to celebrate your book and congratulate yourself for a job well done?
- Is it to promote your business and make more sales?
- Or is it a mixture of all three?

Knowing the reasons behind why you're holding your book launch will help you to make some decisions about it, such as your budget, whether you're charging or offering the event for free, and what's included, so make a note of the purpose before you move on.

It's not just about launching your book, it's about how you can use this opportunity to tell people about it and get people interested in your work.

At this stage I suggest you write down a list of people you'd like to invite to your party as this will influence some of the other points.

The event venue

I've held and attended book launches at very different venues: a private room in a pub in London, hotel conference rooms, a café, community centres, an art space, and a private room in a restaurant in Florence. Before you book your venue, think about what sort of experience you'd like to create. You may choose to have a themed venue, and if so, what type of unusual venue may support this theme? For example, a sporting book would be fitting in a sporting environment, and an art book would be well suited to an arts venue. If a theme is involved, you might also wish to think about how you can dress the room to reflect this.

Do make sure that your venue is fit for purpose. If you'd like to do a presentation as part of your event, make sure that the room is private and that you can hire the relevant equipment (microphone, PA system or projector) if necessary.

The room needs to be big enough for your guests, probably with space for networking and chairs (and maybe tables) if you're giving a talk as part of the event. If you are photographing or videoing the event, allow space for this and think about the lighting. Trust me, I know from experience how important this is!

Remember to be clear on what you want from the venue. Simple things like the layout of the room and space available can make your event less stressful once you're there.

The structure of the event and what's involved

That leads me on to how to structure and time the event. I generally hold my book launch parties in the evening as I believe that more people are likely to be able to attend, but your preferred day and time will probably depend on your readership and what they'd prefer. For example, I spoke at a book launch many years ago which was aimed towards business mums, and it was held at a community centre during the daytime. An evening event would have made it very difficult for this lady's ideal reader to attend.

Plan the structure of the event in advance. Allow time for people to arrive and general networking. If you're giving a talk, plan the time you expect to speak for and what you plan to say, and allow some additional time for questions. If you are doing something different like a raffle, then do allow time for this too. And, most importantly, give yourself time for a book signing as well!

Let me give an example. Say you're holding a book launch party from 7–9pm, then you might wish to allow the first 30 minutes for general networking. Then at 7.30pm you may give a 30-minute talk. After this you could allow 15 minutes for questions. At 8.15pm you can hold a book signing where people can approach you to buy your book. You could close at 8.45pm and thank your guests for coming. Consider having a buffer in your timescales too. For my fourth book launch, we had to leave the venue by a certain time, and the guests were having so much fun, it was hard to persuade everyone to leave!

If you are giving a talk, think about the message that people would like to hear from you. Personally I like to hear the story behind why the book was written, an extract from the book, or some of the tips that are included. This is a great opportunity to showcase your expertise, so do take advantage of it. You may also choose to thank those who have supported you through the process or anyone who has contributed their time or stories.

You may also choose to have guest speakers, but if you do this, they need to be talking about you and your journey and sing your praises. Remember you are the star of the event! It is all about you and your book, not someone else's, and how your book is going to change the lives of your readers!

Your budget

The choice of whether to charge or not for a book launch is up to you and will depend on your budget. There are pros and cons to both. Hiring a venue and including refreshments can be expensive, but if the benefits outweigh the costs – for example you're upselling to a paid-for programme, you're using it as an opportunity to get more business, you know that the PR and publicity is worth the investment, or you simply want to thank your friends and colleagues – then you may want to shoulder the cost yourself.

However you can charge a small fee and make it an attractive proposition for your attendees when you consider what's included in the ticket. As you can see from my experiences, there are many things you can add like a signed copy of your book, branded merchandise, cake, buffet or canapés, a glass of bubbly, soft drinks. The choice is yours.

How to sell tickets for the event and why people should attend

Promoting your event and attracting attendees is crucial, even for a free event. You need to get the word out and let people know that something exciting is happening. Once you have the date set, consider sending a 'save the date' email or postcard well in advance, much in the way you would for a wedding. This ensures that your guests mark their calendars early on. Give yourself ample time to plan and prepare, taking into account the logistics and any necessary arrangements.

Maintaining a record of the expected attendees can greatly assist in managing event numbers. An events management system, which can be used for both free and paid events, proves invaluable for sending invitations, confirming attendance, and keeping a guest list. While there may be a fee associated with using such a system, the benefits it provides, such as efficient guest communication and organised records, make it a worthwhile investment.

Clearly communicate the reasons why people should attend your event. What's in it for them? Whilst many individuals may already be interested in you and eager to learn more about your book, some may require a little more persuasion. Highlight the unique aspects of your event, the experiences they can expect, and the valuable takeaways that await them. Ensuring that attendees understand the benefits they'll receive can enhance their motivation to participate.

Consider various strategies to attract new attendees to your event. Leverage the power of social media platforms, share event details in relevant networking groups, and ask friends to help spread the word. Additionally, you can explore the option of a press release to generate buzz in your local community. Word-of-mouth advertising remains a powerful tool for drawing in new participants and expanding the reach of your event.

Create the wow factor

When creating a memorable event, effective organisation is key. In my case, I've entrusted the organising of my book launch parties to my virtual assistant (now my business manager). Her exceptional skills ensure that everything runs smoothly, allowing me to shine on the day of the event!

If you want to truly create the wow factor, don't shoulder all the responsibilities on your own. Delegate roles to trusted friends and family. Make sure that someone is welcoming your guests when they arrive, whilst another looks after you ensuring you are in the right place at the right time. Having someone to handle book sales, if applicable, can streamline the process.

Think about ways to transform the space and make it visually appealing if necessary. You might incorporate something unusual like a photo booth or relevant accessories that link with your theme. Let me share some other client case studies with you to give you some ideas.

CLIENT STORY
Sheryl Andrews
author of *Manage your Critic – From Overwhelm to Clarity in 7 Steps*

When Sheryl Andrews held her book launch, she added the wow factor. One of her colleagues designed the room for her to make it stand out. She created an amazing showcase for her books, which Sheryl had also used at an exhibition a few days earlier. She dressed the tables and turned the community centre into a book-themed venue that wowed! Having hired a professional photographer, she could use the images from the day as assets for many years post-launch.

CLIENT STORY
Gina Visram
author of *Happily Ever After for Grown-Ups*

I went to Gina's book launch after firstly helping her to finish writing her book, and later helped her with its promotion. She chose a lovely room in a central London pub and it was packed out with well-wishers. Like many of my clients, she had bubbly on arrival, did a talk, and also had a book signing at the event. She used the occasion to thank everyone who'd been part of her journey – and to promote her book!

CLIENT STORY
Louise Evans
author of *5 Chairs, 5 Choices*

I enjoyed travelling to Florence for Louise Evans' book launch party for *5 Chairs, 5 Choices*, which was held in a private room in a beautiful scenic restaurant with bubbly on arrival. She used the opportunity to thank those who had been part of her journey, and as it was just before her first TEDx Talk, she used the opportunity to share her presentation with the audience, and read excerpts from her book. She also had a jazz band and entertained us with a song. She then did a book signing before more wine, canapés, and networking to finish!

Holding an online launch

It would be remiss of me to not mention online launches, because as a result of the COVID-19 pandemic, there were a number of authors who were unable to celebrate their book launches during the lockdown periods. However, these had numerous advantages, most notably enabling authors to connect with a global audience and extend their reach without the need to travel. One client who took advance of this opportunity was Zana Goic Petricevic.

CLIENT STORY
Zana Goic Petricevic
author of *Bold Reinvented*

Zana started working with me on her first book as we went into the COVID-19 pandemic and it was launched 18 months later. Whilst she was able to hold a face-to-face launch in Zagreb, which 70+ people attended, Zana attained a global reach through her online launch.

She organised this launch as an experimental workshop presenting her model and she had other speakers complement her talk and gifts available for attendees. With over 60 people present from all over Europe, Canada, and the US, it was well received by everyone who attended.

How to use a book launch to grow your business

Just like any well-executed event, a book launch party holds immense potential for raising your profile. Consider opportunities for sponsorship, media coverage, or capturing photos or videos that can amplify your brand.

Before my first book launch party, I was interviewed on local TV prior to the event. As I mentioned earlier, I made the most of the opportunity at the launch of my fourth book to have it videoed and turned the clips into YouTube videos to promote my business and my book.

During the event itself, ensure that attendees can purchase your book via card or cash, or if you're charging for the event, allow people to get a copy as part of the ticket price, perhaps offering a discount.

If you plan to have a live book signing on the day, it goes without saying that you need to have an ample supply of books. You may think this is obvious, but for one of my book launches, I only saw the proof copy ten days before my book launch party. This was a little hairy but fortunately we managed to resolve the situation in time for the big day!

Create an inviting atmosphere for a book signing with a nicely decorated table, comfortable chair, quality pen, and think about what you'd like to scribe in the book. In advance of your party, do a practice run or two, so that you know where in the book you are going to sign. If you have already received pre-orders for your book, signing these in advance can save valuable time during the launch.

Don't miss out on other opportunities to engage and assist your guests. How can you help them further? If you plan to offer programmes, workshops, or events which will build on the content in the book, use the launch as a platform to promote these offerings. Consider providing special incentives or exclusive discounts to encourage attendees to sign up.

After the event, follow up with your guests to express your gratitude and request reviews of your book on Amazon and social media platforms, and encourage attendees to share their event photos online.

Remember, your book's launch is just the beginning. Leverage the momentum generated by the event by sharing quotes and testimonials, showcasing captivating photographs and videos, and consistently reminding people how they can buy your book.

 **THINGS TO THINK ABOUT**

Know why you're having your book launch and what you want to get from it. If you write multiple books, you don't have to have multiple book launches, but they are a great way to thank people and raise your books' profile.

Leave enough time from the publication of your book until the book launch. You don't have to hold it immediately. There's nothing worse than worrying whether you're going to have any books!

Bring in the wow factor. There are many low-cost ways to surprise your guests and help them to remember it forever.

Videoing or photographing the event professionally can provide you with great marketing collateral you can use for years to come. You can view the video from my fourth book launch at www.librotas.com/free.

If a physical launch isn't practical or you want a global reach, consider hosting an online launch. Or you could do both!

_____

_____

_____

_____

CHAPTER 17
Bonus book launch tips

It's important to mention in this section that there are other things you can do to launch your book. Whilst they are important the strategies don't each warrant an individual chapter, so consider them a bonus!

Have your book available on all platforms

Just to remind you, although Amazon is the key platform, making sure that your book is available via other means is also important, such as Waterstones, WHSmith and Barnes & Noble. There are various tools available to help you to do this. One of these is Nielsen Books, the organisation that supplies the ISBNs (International Standard Book Numbers) for books in the UK. But they do so much more than this. Book designer Sam Pearce provides her advice on ensuring your book is published wide.

 HOW NIELSEN BOOKS CAN HELP YOU TO ENHANCE YOUR BOOK DISTRIBUTION BY SAMANTHA PEARCE

Nielsen Books are a vital resource for publishers and self-published authors in the UK. They are a leading provider of search, discovery, consumer research, and retail sales analysis tools globally. However more importantly, Nielsen's is the registration agency for ISBN and SAN (Standard Address Numbers) for the UK, Ireland, and all Overseas British Territories. They are responsible for:

- Advising publishers on the correct and proper implementation of the ISBN system.
- Encouraging and promoting the use of the Bookland EAN bar code format (this is the standard EAN-13 barcode with an additional 5-digit add-on supplemental code which contains the suggested retail price).
- Promoting the importance of ISBN numbers in the proper listing of titles with bibliographic agencies.
- Providing technical advice and assistance to publishers, self-published authors, and the wider book trade on all aspects of ISBN usage.

UK ISBN Agency

Registering with Nielsen's as a publisher or self-published author is very straightforward, and can be done online in a matter of minutes. Once your registration is complete you will be allocated a publisher prefix that will form part of the ISBN number for every book you publish. You will then be added to the Publishers' International ISBN Directory (a printed directory of more than 1 million publishers' ISBN prefixes from 221 countries and territories published by De Gruyter Saur) and the Nielsen book publishers' database as a matter of public record.

Your publisher prefix then entitles you to purchase ISBN numbers. As of 2016, Nielsen began to sell ISBN numbers individually, but it is recommended to purchase ISBN numbers in blocks of at least 10. Not only is it more cost effective (£91 for 1 vs. £174 for 10), but also you will require a separate ISBN number for each format of your book. For example, if you plan to release your book as a paperback and an e-book you will require two different ISBN numbers.

More information on ISBN registration and additional support that Nielsen Books can offer you as a self-publishing author can be found at www.nielsenbook.co.uk/isbn-agency. When you are ready to process your registration and purchase your ISBN numbers, you can do so at www.nielsenisbnstore.com.

It is worth noting that many self-publishing platforms such as Amazon KDP and Lulu offer you the use of free ISBNs when using their services. I would recommend NOT doing this, as that platform will be listed as the publisher of record for your book; not you. In addition, though you do not NEED an ISBN number to publish an e-book on Amazon, I would still recommend using one as it will allow you more flexibility in future proofing your book should you wish to make it available via another platform.

Nielsen publisher services

In addition to the allocation and regulation of ISBN numbers, Nielsen's offer a number of additional services to publishers and self-published authors:

Book2Look (www.nielsenisbnstore.com/Home/Book2Look) is a digital marketing tool that can be linked to an individual ISBN number allowing you to market your book more effectively online. Similar to Amazon's 'Look Inside' feature, Book2Look provides your audience with a streamlined presentation of your book with readable excerpts, metadata, reviews, audio and video trailers, and links to preferred retailers. Once a widget is created, it can be posted on a website and fans can share it on blogs and social media networks while you retain control of the content being shared. All reader interactions with your book's widget are logged so you can monitor performance of how and where your book is being shared and how many views it is getting. Cost for the widget varies between £42–£108 per title depending on how many widgets you reserve at any one time.

Nielsen Title Editor (www.nielsentitleeditor.com/titleeditor/) offers a free listing service to all publishers of English language books regardless of location. This service allows you to register basic information about each of your titles, which are then added to the Nielsen Book Database (www.nielsenbook.co.uk/), a database used by retailers and libraries in over 100 countries including Amazon, Waterstones, Bertrams, Gardners, Blackwell, WHSmith, The British Library, Book Depository, eBay, and more. An enhanced listing is also available for an annual fee of £79 that adds additional rich data to up to an individual title listing or £145 for up to 10 listings including a more detailed description, reviews, author biography, and promotional information.

Nielsen BookScan Online (www.online.nielsenbookscan.net/) is a service which collects and reports retail sales information of books and publications from more than 35,500 bookshops across 10 key countries worldwide. This information can be used during the planning stage of your publishing journey to help you determine what to write, the right price to sell it for, and how many to print. Once you have published your book, you can use the service to better understand the demand for your title by reviewing sales performance, and to help you to ensure the book is available during peak selling periods and reduce wholesale returns.

Nielsen recently discontinued their BOSS (BookScan Online Sales Summaries) subscription in favour of a much simpler pay-per-download Lifetime Print Book Sales Data Report. For £108 for the first ISBN and £30 for each additional ISBN (up to a maximum of 10), you will receive a report of the lifetime sales of that ISBN going back to 2001.

Samantha Pearce, SWATT Books, professional self-publishing consultancy. Find out more at www.swatt-books.co.uk.

Note: All quoted prices are correct as of May 2023

If you have taken the independent or self-publishing route, only a few options will allow you to reach worldwide distribution in bookstores, although most will help you to reach a worldwide audience online. You may wish to approach your local bookstores to ask them to stock your book and perhaps arrange a book signing event.

Use Goodreads

Goodreads is another good platform for book lovers, where you can host and promote your book. With over 125 million members, it is owned by Amazon. It provides authors with a great opportunity to showcase their books and connect with fellow authors and readers.

In addition, you can create your author profile, add your blog and/or videos, and interact with readers. You can also list and promote your book, run a giveaway, and advertise your book to their readership.

When you make friends, build relationships, join groups, and give recommendations, then you are more likely to reach like-minded individuals who may be interested in your message.

Hold competitions

Another effective approach is to organise a competition that encourages people to share photos of themselves with your book. This not only increases the visibility of your book but also generates content that can be shared on social media.

However, be mindful of legal considerations, rules and regulations before implementing such a competition.

Here is an example from James Morehen that he started to implement during the pre-launch phase of his first book, which helped him to have a successful launch.

CLIENT STORY
James Morehen
author of *The Performance Nutritionist*

When James wrote his book, he shared his progress regularly via social media, his platform of choice being Instagram. He nurtured people who were interested in the progress of his book, by keeping them up to date with his progress, and developed a buzz before it was published.

As he approached the launch date, he decided to team up with complementary companies to create a prize draw for his book, meaning that if people bought his book directly from his website within the designated launch period and they fulfilled certain criteria (taking a photo of themself with his book, tagging two of their friends and him), they could be in with a chance to win a prize worth £7k.

This led to 200+ copies of his book being sold before his book was launched.

Create a book trailer

A well-designed book trailer can help you to effectively promote your book. A book trailer utilises a combination of voice-overs, music, animation, and live footage to provide essential information about your book in one to two minutes. Surprisingly, book trailers are still relatively underused, making them a worthwhile consideration to promote your book.

When creating a book trailer, consider hiring a skilled videographer or using professional software to ensure high-quality visuals and audios. Craft a compelling script that highlights the unique aspects of your book, leaving viewers eager to find out more.

Complement your book with interviews

Consider complementing your launch with interviews, as this provides valuable opportunities to engage with your audience and extend your reach. If relevant, you could consider conducting interviews with individuals who are featured in your book. I did this when I launched *The Secrets of Successful Coaches*, as previously mentioned.

Interviews can take place in various forms, including podcast appearances, video interviews, radio shows, or written interviews for online publications.

Prepare for interviews by highlighting the key points, anecdotes, and insights from your book that you want to emphasise during the conversation. Consider concise and compelling answers to potential questions that align with your book's messaging and purpose.

Update your profiles

I would like to remind you of the importance of updating your profiles to reflect your new status as a published author. Begin by reviewing your website and consider updating your 'About Me' or 'About the Author' page to include information about your book. This is an opportunity to showcase your achievements and generate interest among your website visitors.

Don't forget to update your bio on social media platforms as well. Update your profiles with your author status and provide a brief description of your book. If you have photographs of yourself with your book, please add them! Regularly share updates about your book's progress, events, and other related news on your social media accounts to keep your audience informed and engaged.

For LinkedIn users, you can add your book publication to your profile. This will enhance your professional presence and allow your connections to easily discover and learn about your work.

Take a comprehensive look at your online presence and identify any relevant organisations, directories, or networking groups you belong to and update your profile there too.

Consider adding your book details to your email signature as well. This simple addition can catch the attention of recipients and serve as a subtle promotion whenever you correspond via email.

Create a plan!

In addition to profile updates, revisit the pre-launch strategies discussed earlier in this book. Evaluate which strategies align with the platforms you use and select the ones that work best for you. Create a concrete plan to execute these strategies, ensuring that you leverage various channels and platforms to promote your book effectively.

That's it for the launch section. Which actions are you going to take? Doing all of these will help you to get your book noticed, but make sure you have the time to do them well. Next, we will focus on how you can maintain momentum and continue to build your business through your book.

 **THINGS TO THINK ABOUT**

Use every opportunity to promote your book and remember to continue using some of the suggestions I made in the pre-launch section.

Having a consistent message about your book will lead to new opportunities that you may have never expected.

Don't underestimate the power of your existing contacts who can help you to promote your book and get it out to more people.

Consider implementing strategies that not many other people are using as this will help you to stand out further.

Take a moment now to review what you've learnt from this section. Which options are you going to choose to create a buzz for your book when you launch it?

_____

_____

_____

_____

_____

_____

SECTION 3:
POST-LAUNCH PROMOTION

When you reach this stage, you might be thinking, "Phew. I've launched my book, what happens next?"

After launching your book, the journey doesn't end. In fact, it's just the beginning. The ongoing marketing and promotion of your book are essential for it to truly benefit your business. If you simply publish it and do nothing more, it will remain stagnant and fail to contribute to your growth.

Time is of the essence, as your book has a shelf life. Depending on its content, the information you've shared may become outdated over time. Whilst you can release a second edition or add new content later (like I have done with this book), maintaining your motivation for promotion now is crucial to staying on track.

Whilst receiving royalties is fantastic, the ultimate goal is for your book to serve as a catalyst for income generation through various means. By continuing to demonstrate your credibility and expertise, your book should pave the way for attracting clients and valuable opportunities. When you witness your book successfully contributing to your business's growth, you know you're on the right track!

CHAPTER 18
Dive into digital and audio

It is essential to adapt to the evolving reading habits and preferences of your audience. Whilst holding a physical copy of your book remains a cherished experience, by complementing your print book with digital and audio versions, you can cater to a diverse range of readers and learners.

In this chapter, I will delve further into the realm of digital and audio book production, providing valuable insights and practical tips.

Whilst this chapter sits in the post-launch section of this book, you may well consider both of these options alongside your book launch.

Create a digital version of your book

Digital books provide numerous benefits, including portability and immediate access for readers. As I mentioned earlier, one of the most popular platforms for e-books is Amazon's Kindle, which allows you to reach a wide audience. However, it's important to explore other platforms as well, such as Apple Books, Kobo Writing Life, Barnes & Noble Press (formerly Nook), Smashwords, Draft2Digital, among others, to maximise your book's visibility.

To ensure a seamless reading experience, it is crucial to properly format your e-book. Avoid uploading a Word version or PDF, as these often contain embedded formatting and images that don't convert well to e-books. Instead, consider hiring a professional e-book designer or using e-book conversion software to create industry-standard formats such as EPUB or MOBI.

Publishing your e-book on Amazon Kindle is a straightforward process. Begin by creating an account on Amazon Kindle Direct Publishing (KDP) and navigate to the Bookshelf section. There, you can add essential details about your book, including the title, subtitle, description, keywords, and categories. Next, upload your cover design and the properly formatted e-book file. You will also need to set the price for your e-book and choose between a 35% or 70% royalty option based on factors like book price and distribution terms.

Consider exploring Amazon KDP Select, which offers additional promotional opportunities and inclusion in Kindle Unlimited and Kindle Owners' Lending Library. However, enrolling in KDP Select requires exclusivity, meaning you will not be able to add your e-book to any of the other mentioned platforms during the exclusivity period.

You have flexibility in creating your e-book. You can choose to create it before, alongside, after, or instead of a physical book. Here is another client's story.

CLIENT STORY
Gina Visram
author of *Happily Ever After for Grown-Ups*

One of my business clients, Gina Visram, launched her first book in 2014 with my support, but at the time she hadn't published a Kindle version of her book. Later she came back to me to get marketing support for her book and use it to increase her visibility.

To create a buzz for her book, with my support, she crafted an Amazon launch for her Kindle book. She decided to put together an offer to give it away for free over the Valentine's weekend in 2015 (which worked well with her book's content). This helped her to reach number one on Amazon in her category and re-energised the sales of her physical book.

Additionally, you may consider writing a shorter e-book as a standalone work or as a teaser for a more comprehensive book, as discussed in chapter 3 in Helen Monaghan's example.

As also mentioned in chapter 3, I did something similar in 2022, when I launched my ninth book, *The 7 Shifts*. I decided to initially launch it as a digital book only as a low-cost lead magnet with a funnel to encourage readers to take further action and sign up for other programmes. This digital book is still a full-length book and is a good introduction to my services because it lays out the process you need to follow before you start to actually write your book if you want it to use it to attract more clients and engage a new audience. I decided to host it on my website and it is currently available as a flipbook via Designrr.com rather than Amazon to allow flexibility for updates and revisions. You can find out more at www.the7shifts.com.

Create an audio version of your book

In today's fast-paced environment, audiobooks have become increasingly popular, offering a convenient way for people to consume books while on the go. By creating an audio version of your book, you can make it more accessible to a broader audience and provide an alternative reading experience.

There are several options for using audio in your book strategy. You may choose to create an audio version of a portion or an abridged version of your book, offering it as a free sample on your website or through platforms like iTunes. This allows potential readers to get a taste of your book and encourages them to explore it further.

Another option is to produce a complete audio recording of your book, which can be made available for purchase on platforms such as Audible. Audible, an Amazon subsidiary, offers the Audiobook Creation Exchange (ACX) platform for authors to publish their audiobooks. By uploading your audiobook to ACX, it will be distributed through Audible, Amazon, and iTunes, increasing your book's visibility and potential sales. Royalties of 25–40% can be earned on audiobook sales through these platforms.

It's worth noting that audiobook listeners often overlap with readers of physical books, so offering an audio version can be an effective way to boost overall sales. By providing multiple formats, you cater to different preferences and attract a wider range of readers.

Additionally, you have the option to create an audio-only version of your book. This approach can be explored using platforms like Findaway Voices, which offer hosting and distribution services to major audiobook platforms. I did this as an experiment when I launched my sixth book, *Becoming An Authority.* I did this because many of my clients were asking about whether they needed to have an audiobook so I wanted to learn about the process.

How to record your audiobook

I recorded *Becoming An Authority* at Igloo Studios near me in Hampshire. It took two half-days to record the book which was around 37,000 words at the time. As I used the professional studio, one of their team was editing the recording as we went, so whenever I fell over my words, we took the recording back a sentence or two and then did a retake. Of which there were many! A week or so later, I had the recordings in the right format to upload to the distribution site. I documented the process at the time, and you can find out more at www.librotas.com/free. If you go to Findaway Voices, you can purchase the audiobook.

Prior to this, in 2016, I recorded the introduction of my third book, *Your Book is the Hook*, which we used as part of its promotion. You can listen to the introduction at www.librotas.com/free.

Although there is an inherent cost to recording your book in a professional studio, if you want a high-quality result, then having a budget for your audio recording is essential.

I recently interviewed Elliott Frisby from Monkeynut Audiobooks for my Smart Author – Fast Track and Community members and I have extracted some of his wisdom on why creating an audiobook is a perfect addition to your print book.

 SEVEN THINGS TO THINK ABOUT BEFORE RECORDING AND LAUNCHING YOUR AUDIOBOOK BY ELLIOTT FRISBY

Audiobook consumption is on the rise due to people's busy lifestyles and the convenience of listening on the go. It also provides anonymity for readers of self-help books who may not want others to know what they are reading. Here are seven things to think about before you record and launch your audiobook.

1. Launch your audiobook simultaneously with the release of your physical book. If readers are interested in your content but prefer audio format, delaying the audiobook release may cause them to lose interest and forget about your work.

2. Avoid recording your audiobook yourself as a cost-saving measure. Quality is crucial, and a poor first impression can deter listeners. It's important to have a professionally produced audiobook with minimal background noise and high production values.

3. Similar to readers checking out book blurbs, potential listeners often listen to a 3–5-minute sample before deciding to purchase an audiobook. If the sample fails to meet their expectations, they may skip buying it or even leave negative reviews.

4. While hiring a professional narrator is a great option, if you want to be the voice of your book, we offer training to improve your narration skills. Ensuring that your performance is exceptional and engaging is crucial to creating a phenomenal audiobook.

5. Consider marketing strategies that include bonus interviews with the author. As part of our package, we arrange professionally filmed interviews which can be used as high-quality video content to promote the audiobook on social media platforms. This additional content can also justify a higher price for the audiobook.

6. Although you can exclusively publish your audiobook on Audible, I advise you to take a non-exclusive approach (even though this will reduce your Audible royalty percentage). When you choose non-exclusive distribution, you can publish it on all the other audiobook download sites, which will give you a larger audience. Many of these download sites are already doing well and on the rise.

7. Recognise that audiobooks are a long-term investment. Once recorded, they remain available for listeners to access indefinitely. Treat your audiobook as part of your legacy and strive to make it exceptional and memorable.

Elliott Frisby is the founder of Monkeynut Audiobooks, one of the UK's leading and respected audiobook creators. With 25+ years' experience, he specialises in creating audiobooks that keep people listening. Find out more about Elliott at www.monkeynutuk.com.

Prepare your voice for audio

When I recorded the audiobook for *Becoming An Authority*, one really helpful bit of advice I received from Dielle Hannah, co-owner of Igloo Studios, was to prepare my voice first. She gave me voice exercises and other hints and tips, and she has also shared her thoughts here. Most recently, she has recorded an audiobook on this topic.

FIVE TIPS FOR RECORDING A GOOD VOICE-OVER BY DIELLE HANNAH

Delivering your voice-over well can make your project and cut down on editing time. Here are top tips to ensure your voice-over session goes well.

1. Be familiar with your script

Being sure about what you are saying will help you feel relaxed, and deliver the script fluidly.

2. Enunciate

We know – it's not cool. But speaking clearly, with correct pronunciation, ensures that your script will be clear alongside background music or sound effects.

3. Slow down

Most of us think much faster than we speak, and speak much faster than is necessary for a good voice-over. Breathe, stay calm and slow down. Your words per minute will reflect the mood of your project, however the BBC recommend a broadcasting rate of 160–180 words per minute for radio, which can be used as a guide.

4. Modulate

Don't be too shy to be a bit more tuneful than you would be in everyday speech. Explore your natural higher and lower tones and how they suit your script.

5. Speak confidently

Being well prepared as in tip number 1 will help you avoid hesitation, ums and ahs. Own your space, know your project, and deliver with confidence.

Dielle Hannah is the author of *Voice Care and Training for Speakers*, which is available as an audiobook. For more information about recording your audiobook at Igloo Studios, go to www.igloomusic.co.uk.

One final thing to mention in this chapter is that use of your material is not just confined to your book. When you self-publish particularly, you'll retain the intellectual property to your work. This means that you can use the material again and again in products, programmes, webinars, and any way in which you'd like to promote your business and your book. And I'm sure you already know my philosophy – repurpose, repurpose, and repurpose! More about this next.

THINGS TO THINK ABOUT

Different people like to process information in different ways, which is why I suggest you have digital and audio versions of your book. This allows you to reach more people than those who may read a physical book, and some may even buy all three!

When publishing your e-book, although it is worth listing your book on Amazon Kindle, consider the other options out there to extend your reach.

You can choose to publish an audiobook at any stage; there are advantages of doing it alongside your physical book launch and you may choose to do it later on, which can reinvigorate sales of your book.

You don't have to record your whole book in audio format. You could choose to record the first chapter to give people an introduction in the early stages or a sample to pique your reader's interest.

Think about investing in your book. In creating a digital book, use a specialist book designer as this will give you the best possible result. Hire a professional studio for your audiobook as this will mean that you have a good quality recording that allows you to stand out.

_____

_____

CHAPTER 19
Produce products and programmes

Earlier in this book, I talked about your reader's journey and knowing where you might take your reader next as being one of the crucial elements of your book's production.

Whilst some readers will read your book and take action, there will be others who read it and do nothing. If they desire additional and ongoing support, then it makes sense to offer this to them. This is where your products and programmes come in.

In addition, it allows you to further build your business from your content. And whilst it is ideal to have them in place before you launch your book, you may find yourself developing more comprehensive programmes after your launch.

And if you find yourself unable to scale because you are constantly working one-to-one with clients, I strongly recommend this option. The following examples from my own business demonstrate its significance.

In the summer of 2014, whilst writing *Your Book is the Hook*, I created a low-cost online programme. I sold it through a series of three free Q&A style webinars. Then I created and ran the programme, and wrote the book alongside delivering the webinars. The programme allowed me to write the bulk of the book, which meant that I was able to write it quickly. I went from idea to book publication in six months.

Additionally, the programme provided real-time feedback from clients, helping me to refine and develop the content. It allowed me to reach a broader audience interested in working with me personally. It generated £16,000 in income in a short period of time through programme sign-ups, new one-to-one and writing retreat clients, and pre-sales of the book. All before I'd published it.

When I launched the first edition of this book in 2017, I ran a 30-day Book Marketing Challenge as part of the launch. This challenge, which is still available for purchase on my website, offers detailed guidance on book marketing through webinars, interviews, and by generating publicity for your book.

In 2019, I published *Becoming An Authority* as an audiobook, just before the start of the COVID-19 pandemic. Given the circumstances, instead of turning the audiobook into a physical book, it led to the creation of the Smart Author System programme, which was up and running within six weeks with dedicated effort and support from my team.

Anticipating that more people would use their time during lockdown to write their books and potentially faced financial hardships, I aimed to provide an affordable and comprehensive resource. Over time, this online programme evolved into three levels: Self-study, Community, and Fast Track, each catering to different levels of support and engagement. At the time of updating this book, over 100 people have participated or are currently enrolled in the programme.

As I mentioned in the introduction, the unique aspect of the Smart Author System is the focus on how to self-fund a book, a concept explored further in the second edition of this book. By following the programme, individuals can reap the rewards of becoming an author even before publishing it.

To complement the Smart Author System, in 2021 I produced the *Business Book Planner* and *Book Writing Journal*. These low-content books have been designed to accompany the Smart Author System. To support this book, I have created the *Book Marketing Planner*. All can be purchased directly from Amazon to help support your book planning, writing, and marketing journey.

How to develop your product or programme

When thinking about running a programme and writing a book, a question that many people ask me is this: What is the difference between the product or programme and the book? In my view, a product is likely to be more bespoke than a book, especially when you include access to yourself in the form of webinars or an online forum (or both), and you may also choose to add one-to-one or group support as part of your package.

To develop your product or programme, the best approach is to align its content with your book. You may choose to delve deeper into specific topics or offer an overview of the whole process. I have personally employed both approaches.

When promoting your product or programme, preview webinars can be effective, where you provide valuable content and then offer an upsell to the programme. Promote to your mailing list and social media platforms to reach your target audience. Additionally, consider employing Facebook advertising to expand your reach.

To effectively promote your offering, you'll need a sales page on your website and a seamless payment system similar to the one described earlier for pre-selling your book. Address the problems your clients are facing and clearly articulate how your programme provides solutions. Incorporating client testimonials as social proof and providing a clear call to action will enhance your promotional efforts.

After delivering the programme, offer participants the next stage of engagement if they wish to continue working with you. Make sure to communicate how they can access further support. Gathering feedback and testimonials from your clients will serve as valuable endorsements for future promotions.

While having a dedicated membership platform for your programme is ideal, starting with a password-protected hidden page on your website for paid content is a budget-friendly option.

You can also consider other possibilities for creating products, such as:

- Creating an online programme with a series of videos or audios for self-paced learning, which is available as an evergreen product.
- Offering an information product, like a recorded course, that guides readers to the next steps.
- Establishing a membership club to provide ongoing support and generate recurring income.
- Organising events, workshops, or retreats that complement your book's theme.
- Providing one-on-one support for readers seeking personalised guidance.
- Developing a workbook that readers can complete alongside your book.

I worked with Naomi Jane Johnson to create the aforementioned *Business Book Planner* and *Book Writing Journal* that accompany my Smart Author System and I have asked her to share her thoughts on this topic.

HOW COMPANION BOOKS CAN COMPLEMENT YOUR BUSINESS BOOK BY NAOMI JANE JOHNSON

Once your book is written and 'out there', it's time to consider all possible options for marketing and promoting to the target audience of people most likely to purchase.

One strategy that you may not have considered is creating a 'companion' book – for example a journal, planner, or workbook – to complement your business book.

These are generally known as low-content books and have become popular over the last few years. Books such as journals, planners, and workbooks could potentially be a valuable supplementary resource, serving as an essential companion that enhances the learning experience.

Let's take a look at why incorporating a journal, planner, or workbook is a worthwhile exercise for authors seeking to maximise the benefits of their business book.

Active engagement and application

A journal, planner, or workbook actively encourages readers to engage with the content of the business book. By providing designated spaces for reflection, note-taking, and exercises, these tools prompt readers to grasp key concepts and relate them to their personal circumstances. This interactive approach helps to facilitate the practical application of ideas presented in the book, allowing readers to translate theory into action.

Reinforcement and retention

Supplementary tools act as reinforcement mechanisms, aiding readers in retaining knowledge gained from the business book. Writing down important points, summarising chapters, and completing exercises helps cement key ideas in readers' minds, making them more likely to remember and apply the concepts well after they have finished reading. The repetitive process of writing and reviewing strengthens neural connections, enhancing learning and comprehension.

Goal setting and progress tracking

A planner or workbook offers an excellent platform for setting goals and tracking progress. It offers an opportunity to align the insights from the business book with their personal objectives. By breaking down larger goals into actionable steps, readers can plan their journey to success and monitor progress along the way. This combination of strategic planning and accountability boosts the chance of achieving desired outcomes.

Long-term reference and review

The combined use of a journal, planner, or workbook with a business book creates a valuable long-term reference. Readers can revisit their notes, reflections, and exercises at any time, refreshing their understanding of the material and extracting new insights. This ongoing process ensures that the knowledge gained from the book remains top of mind and applicable in various contexts, contributing to continuous professional and personal development.

Conclusion

Journals, planners, and workbooks are valuable complements to a business book. These supplementary tools promote active engagement, aid in goal setting, personalise the experience, and serve as long-term references.

Together, the business book and its companion low-content book create a powerful combination that facilitates readers' understanding and learning experience.

Naomi Jane Johnson is a self-employed digital designer with particular expertise in creating low-content books. She offers a comprehensive range of affordable design-based products, services, and training. You can find out more at www.naomijanejohnson.co.uk.

Remember your value

Having confidence in charging what you're worth and increasing your fees to reflect the value you offer is essential. One client of mine experienced delight when she increased her fees after starting to write her book, as people began paying without hesitation. She also transformed her service delivery by offering packaged services instead of one-off sessions, resulting in increased income.

Adding value to your programmes is crucial. For instance, in our writing retreat in Spain, we provide mentoring before attendees fly to Spain, access to online materials, support during the retreat, and follow-up assistance upon their return. This comprehensive approach ensures participants get the most out of their time and investment. You can find more details about our retreats at www.writingretreats.co.uk.

Having programmes available at different levels and price points allows individuals to access your knowledge in a way that aligns with their preferences and budget. Some may prefer group support, while others may opt for one-on-one interactions.

Let me share some client examples.

CLIENT STORY
Emma Heptonstall
author of *How To Be A Lady Who Leaves: The Ultimate Guide to Getting Divorce-Ready*

Emma's book was first published in 2017 and is now in its second edition. In a very narrow niche, Emma is the host of The Six Minute Divorce podcast and the UK's first online membership for divorcing women, The Absolute Academy, both of which have grown since the publication of her book.

This book is not a substitute for legal advice, but it sits nicely alongside it. It's endorsed by family lawyers who recommend it to their clients. When a client understands what they should discuss with their lawyer and what is best shared with a friend/coach or therapist they will literally save themselves thousands of pounds – and that has always been Emma's passion, which she achieves through her book and her monthly membership academy.

CLIENT STORY
Sarah Hamilton-Gill FCIPD
author of *Leap Into HR Consulting*

Sarah Hamilton-Gill FCIPD wrote her book to introduce readers to her process and way of working. To complement her book, she offers a bootcamp that supports them as they set up their HR consulting business. At the time of writing this client story, she had supported over 135 clients through her bootcamp and many more have been coached on a one-to-one basis or attended her retreat in Corfu.

Remember, as your business and team grow, your offerings will also evolve. Embrace the process and continually seek opportunities to serve your audience more effectively.

THINGS TO THINK ABOUT

You can write your book and then create your product after you've published or develop it alongside writing your book.

Think about how you can support your readers after they've read your book and the journey they might consider taking with you.

Recognise the value of what you offer and develop your products and programmes based on what your clients want from you.

Your product or programme could be a workbook, online programme, event, workshop, retreat, or membership, to name a few different options.

Develop the confidence to charge what you're worth and package everything that you do. This will add value and help you to support your clients.

_____

_____

_____

_____

_____

CHAPTER 20
Step into successful speaking

When planning the launch of your book, one strategy I highly recommend to my clients is lining up speaking engagements. Whilst it may be challenging to find time for speaking during the writing phase, once you have a physical book to promote and sell, they offer an excellent opportunity to connect with your audience. These engagements can take various forms, including live events, online summits, interviews, and podcasts, as discussed earlier in the book.

In this chapter, I will share effective strategies to help you develop, refine, and deliver your message while finding the perfect speaking engagements that align with your goals. By implementing these strategies, you can make the most of your book launch and engage directly with your readers and potential clients.

Get clear on your topic and message

Before diving into the topic of how to get speaking engagements, it's important to get clarity on the message you want to convey and your ideal audience. You need to decide which part of your book you want to talk about, otherwise you may have a very long talk! If your book is a step-by-step guide, consider selecting a specific part of your system to discuss during your talk whilst alluding to the other parts in your book. Alternatively, you could give an overview of your system and specific examples. If your book is memoir style, share captivating stories from your experiences and what you have learnt.

Once you have a clear idea of your topic and message, the next step is to create a speaker profile. This one-page PDF document is a valuable tool to share with event organisers who handle speaking engagements. The speaker profile should highlight key aspects of your talk and essential information. Consider including the following details:

- The title of your talk and your name.
- A concise summary outlining the purpose and target audience of your talk.
- 3–5 bullet points that succinctly describe what attendees will get from your presentation.
- Any additional relevant information about your session.
- A brief biography (2–3 paragraphs) showcasing your expertise and mentioning your book.
- A professional photograph of yourself and, if applicable, the cover of your book.
- Relevant reviews from previous talks or satisfied clients.

For a sample speaker profile, go to www.librotas.com/free.

I recommend creating two or three different speaker profiles that provide variety in your presentations whilst remaining focused on the core topic of your book.

Get speaking engagements

Now that you have your speaker profile ready, it's time to use it to find speaking engagements. Here are some strategies to help you to secure opportunities aligned with your target readers and clients:

Identify your target audience and their gathering places: Consider the profile of your ideal reader and client. Think about where they are likely to gather, such as industry-specific events, conferences, coaching groups, or networking events. For example, if you work with coaches and small business owners, speaking at coaching groups or relevant conferences can be effective.

Contact event organisers: Once you have identified the groups or events where your target audience can be found, reach out to the person responsible for organising the speakers. Visit their website to understand their preferred approach and follow their guidelines when contacting them. Be professional and concise in your communication, highlighting the value you can bring to their event.

Leverage social media: If you are unsure where to start or want to broaden your search, consider posting on social media that you are actively seeking speaking engagements. Clearly state what you are looking for to attract relevant opportunities. This approach can yield positive results, but ensure you are specific to avoid wasting time on irrelevant enquiries.

Showcase your book: Once your book is published, consider sending a copy to event organisers. This not only grabs their attention but also serves as a powerful way to showcase your work and expertise. It can increase the chances of securing speaking engagements.

Understand the compensation landscape: In the early stages, you may find yourself speaking for free, with travel or refreshment expenses covered. However, if you have permission to sell your books and offer additional products or services, such as a book signing or special deals, you can recoup your investment. As you gain experience and recognition, don't hesitate to negotiate payment for your speaking engagements, taking into account factors like travel time and accommodation expenses. I remember once speaking to one of my clients who was getting advice on how much to charge for a speaking gig. Although it was a short speaking slot, it required her to travel over 5000 miles and readjust to the time zone, so the quote wasn't cheap!

Consider joining a speaker bureau: If speaking engagements are a core part of your business and you are seeking high-profile paid opportunities, joining a speaker bureau may be beneficial. These agencies can help you access keynote speeches and other sought-after speaking engagements, acting as intermediaries to connect you with suitable opportunities.

I've travelled all around the UK for speaking engagements, because it has allowed me to travel and meet interesting groups of people. Speaking enables me to connect with some lovely clients and some have worked with me personally.

Of course, it's important to note that since 2020 the speaking environment has changed. With many networking groups connecting online, you don't necessarily need to leave the comfort of your office to speak to audiences all around the world. Some networking companies are solely online now, and others have hybrid options, meaning that you can speak to massive audiences via Zoom. I'll talk more about this in a moment.

To enhance your chances of securing speaking engagements and generate business from your talks, consider the following on your website:

- Create a dedicated page to list your speaking engagements, and provide a clear booking link should an interested event organiser wish to have a conversation with you.
- Include a video showreel showcasing you in action as a speaker.
- Display professional photographs of you speaking, adding visual appeal to your page.
- Incorporate testimonials from previous attendees or clients, highlighting the impact of your speaking engagements.

How to structure and deliver your talk

Whilst this book isn't solely focused on giving talks, I'd like to provide some key considerations to help you deliver impactful presentations. For more in-depth guidance and support in honing your speaking skills and delivery, I recommend seeking assistance from experts in this field.

To capture the attention of your audience from the start, draw inspiration from the examples I have discussed throughout this book. The 4MAT process, which I explored in *Your Book is the Hook*, can be applied to planning and delivering your talk. This framework allows you to engage your audience and cater to their different learning needs. Incorporating stories is an effective way to captivate your listeners while authentically sharing your knowledge and experiences.

The advantage of preparing talks based on your book is that you already have valuable content at your disposal. There is no need to come up with entirely new material. However, for each presentation, it is essential to establish clear outcomes that guide your talk, allocate time for questions, and inform the audience of the next steps or actions you'd like them to take.

Let me consider here unique aspects of delivering talks online. Firstly, it's useful to familiarise yourself with the platforms for online speaking engagements. Ensure you have a stable internet connection, suitable equipment (microphone, webcam), and a distraction-free environment. If you are using slides, liaise with the organisers beforehand because it can be particularly frustrating if the first 60 seconds are wasted with a speaker trying to work out how to share their screen!

To maintain audience engagement during online talks, consider incorporating interactive elements. You may consider using the chat features, polling tools, or breakout rooms to encourage participation and interaction. Incorporate visuals, such as slides or multimedia, to enhance the virtual experience and reinforce key points, though keep them simple.

Although it's always crucial to capture your audience's attention early, it is particularly important when delivering an online talk. Begin with a compelling hook or story that captures them from the outset. Leverage visuals, storytelling techniques, and dynamic delivery to maintain engagement throughout your presentation.

How to get leads and sales from your talks

Lastly, the purpose of any talk – unless you have been briefed otherwise – is to give great content that engages and excites your audience, but there are ways in which you can use them to obtain valuable leads and clients.

Get permission to promote: If your speaking engagement is in person, get permission to promote your books, do a book signing, or mention special offers. If online, share a link of how people can easily order your book. There may be the option for promotion, though you are likely to pay commission to the organiser.

Bundle books into your speaker fee: If your talk is for an organisation or group who have engaged you, consider bundling copies of your book into your speaker fee. This can add huge value to the recipients, enhance your talk, and enable you to charge a higher fee.

Obtain contact details: Provide a valuable bonus for attendees that will require them to provide their contact details, such as a lead magnet, checklist, or something related to your book. This will allow you to stay connected and enable you to nurture the relationship after the event. You may also encourage connecting with attendees on social media platforms.

By implementing these strategies and optimising your online presence, you can position yourself as a sought-after speaker and maximise the impact of your speaking engagements.

Let me end this chapter with a client story from Nick Fewings, who has delivered on all of these principles since launching his book in 2022. You can see what he has achieved by incorporating speaking into his core business plan.

CLIENT STORY
Nick Fewings
author of *Team Lead Succeed*

Nick recently shared with me some of his successes in terms of post-launch strategies to promote his book, *Team Lead Succeed*, in March 2022. When I sought his feedback in April 2023, he told me that – as a result of writing and publishing his book – he has seen a 66% increase in business.

The majority of this has been new business in terms of new clients. In addition, seeing his book mentioned on social media has also resulted in previous clients seeking new work from him.

Linking in specifically with this chapter, Nick was asked and paid to be a keynote speaker at a conference for leaders from throughout Northern Europe, and additionally they bought 175 copies of his book (one for each delegate).

This leads me to another success that Nick shared with me. In addition to Amazon sales, he has sold 650 books directly at conferences and to his team development clients. This backs up my earlier point. Although it's important to promote your book online, when you sell your book directly to your readers then this adds value to your event and boosts your book sales.

 **THINGS TO THINK ABOUT**

Don't wait until your book is published to get speaking engagements as high-quality speaking gigs are usually booked up many months in advance.

Create your speaker profile, which sells you and your expertise, and have a couple of options that would appeal to different audiences and topics.

Consider whether you want to give talks at in-person events or online, or both, and tailor your approach accordingly.

Have a speaker showreel or video on your website which shows you in action and some photographs of you giving a talk.

Consider how you can leverage your talks to create more leads and sell (or bundle) copies of your book.

CHAPTER 21
Maintain momentum

Many people struggle to keep their book visible and relevant long after its initial release and I will explore some of these techniques to help you do that in this chapter. By leveraging the strategies covered earlier in this book, such as encouraging reviews and speaking at events, along with these additional methods, you can maintain momentum, extend the lifespan of your book and maximise its impact. Let's dive in and discover simple and easy ways to promote your book over the months and years to come.

Take your book with you everywhere

A really simple and free thing that you can do is to take your book with you when you are doing anything related to your business. This specifically includes networking events where it's a great prop for your elevator pitch, trade fairs or exhibitions, meetings with a prospective client or contact, or anywhere you might meet your ideal clients and readers. Keep a copy in your car, so there is always a book not too far away if you need it!

Even on virtual events, why not hold up your book if there is a photo opportunity that is likely to be shared on social media after the event. Or have a Zoom background that shows a copy of your book (and perhaps include a QR code to make it easy for someone to order it!).

Give away your book

If you're using your book as an 'expensive business card' to attract new business, don't be afraid to give it away. Although it might cost you a few pounds every time you do it, if you get one piece of business from giving away your book or help one new person, then it will most definitely be worth it.

You may give a copy of your book to a prospective client, send a copy with an introductory letter to a corporate contact as lumpy mail, or use it to help you get a speaking engagement. You also may pop a copy in the post to a journalist contact, as they may want to review your book before they write about it.

If you'd like to get some brilliant reviews for your book, then it is definitely worth sending copies to people who are influential in your industry, as people will buy your book based on the social proof of what others say. Write a list of people who you'd like to get your book in front of, and then send them a copy with an appropriate covering letter. And, most importantly, follow up!

It's become common for experts and influencers to launch their book and give their book away as a lead magnet on their website. In return for your name, email, and address, they only charge for the physical cost of packaging and posting it. This means that they capture your information and can promote their products to you, and you receive a valuable piece of information that doesn't get lost in your emails, which may well lead to you becoming their client! Could you do the same?

Attend trade fairs, expos, or exhibitions

One of the ways to get in front of your ideal clients is to go where they hang out. You might choose to have a stand, sponsor an exhibition, secure a guest speaker spot, or attend as a guest.

If you can, get a copy of the guest list or exhibition list in advance and know who you would like to speak with, and why. Take copies of your book, a pile of business cards and remember to follow up.

During the final edits of the first edition of this book, I was approached by Angela de Souza to attend her Women's Business Club's Maximise Conference and have a stand in her author hub. My books had previously raised my profile, so we'd already connected, and I knew it was a worthwhile thing to do. I was featured alongside other well-known speakers, so it was worth doing it to raise my profile. This type of event also gives you great PR and you can use videos and photos to share on your socials.

Seek opportunities

As a published author, you have the opportunity to extend your reach in so many ways. I have already mentioned seeking interviews, guest blog or podcast opportunities, and whilst they may not offer monetary compensation, the exposure and engagement they provide make them valuable promotional opportunities.

Personally, I have been approached to contribute to other books, provide guest blogs, contribute to online summits, speak at a multi-speaker event, present for someone's membership audience, and dozens of podcast and live interviews and webinars.

You could also considering doing a TEDx Talk. I did a TEDx not long after publishing the first edition of this book, although the topic was based on my fourth book, *The Mouse That Roars*, because it fitted in with the theme for the event.

Many of my clients have also done TEDx Talks because they are a great way to spread great ideas, hone your message into less than 18 minutes, and provide another accolade to add to your website and social media channels.

You don't have to wait for collaboration opportunities to be presented to you. You could initiate events yourself. Consider running your own event, conference, summit, or programme. One example I mentioned earlier is when I launched my second book at my own 'Star Biz' conference where I had seven other amazing speakers and we did a firewalk at the event, making it memorable.

Consider local media outreach

Consider contacting local newspapers, radio stations, or television channels to pitch your book for potential interviews, features, or reviews. Local media outlets are often interested in showcasing local authors and their work.

Use online advertising

You can promote your book via Facebook, Google Ads, YouTube, among many other platforms. I've used Facebook advertising as part of promotions for lead magnets and low-cost books as part of a marketing funnel.

There are also various book-related platforms to consider in terms of advertising. Although I have not used it personally, one to consider is BookBub. Using their targeted email campaigns and promotional tools, you can showcase your work to their audience through discounted deals, free promotions, or targeted advertising.

And, of course, let's not forget Amazon Advertising, which has become a particularly effective avenue for promoting non-fiction books. With precise targeting options, you can reach individuals actively searching for knowledge and information on specific topics. By leveraging sponsored product ads, you can increase your book's visibility, attract new readers, and drive sales.

If you undertake any kind of advertising, I recommend working with an expert or undertaking training, as it's easy to waste money if you don't track your ad's performance and tweak the campaign regularly.

Offer affiliate programmes and joint ventures

Another thing to consider is having affiliate programmes or joint ventures for books or programmes, which I mentioned briefly earlier in this book. There are many ways in which this can work to the mutual benefit of both parties. Your book or programme may benefit one of your colleagues and vice versa. If you are inviting other people to contribute to your book or programme, then inviting them to share it with their community will have mutual benefits.

In 2016 I was approached by a contact for a bulk order of my books that she could sell at one of her events. This is a great way to get in front of more people and it benefited both of us. This is a strategy that many of my clients follow. If you have published your book via a publish on demand platform, books can be shipped directly to your readers.

Host webinars and masterclasses

Just to remind you, be proactive with the promotion of your book. Don't wait for other people to promote you to get your book out there. At any stage you can run webinars – see chapter 7 for more information on this topic. I regularly run webinars that enable me to add great value to my community. Sometimes I may be promoting an event and other times I'm simply building my list and telling people how I can help them further.

With some of my events, where I've had speakers, I've used this as part of my promotion. It's a great way to introduce my speakers to my community, have them promote me to their community, and also to shape the content of the events. I also run regular masterclasses for my Smart Author Community and Fast Track members as they can tap into my network, and I can keep them up to date with emerging trends or answer their questions via an interactive call.

Hold book offers

At any time during your book's publication you can do promotions and offers for your book or other services. Special offers or including your book as a bonus on a programme are all great ways to raise your profile and bring in additional income. You could offer discounts if people buy books in bulk for their colleagues or friends. Or if you have more than one book, you could offer a discount if people purchase multiple books from you.

Embrace collaborative marketing

Connect with other authors in your genre and explore collaborative marketing opportunities. This could include joint promotions, cross-promotions in newsletters, or bundling your books together for a limited-time offer.

You could also collaborate with influencers or bloggers who have a substantial following in your book's target audience. Offer them a free copy of your book and propose a collaboration, such as an interview, guest blog post, or social media shoutout.

Enter business or book awards

You may choose to submit your business or book for relevant awards or contests. Winning or being nominated for an award can provide significant exposure and boost your book's credibility.

There are lots of options to enter and win awards. I was the winner of the Women's Business Club Creative Business of the Year award in 2017 and a few of my clients have been finalists in the Business Book Awards. Here is one example.

CLIENT STORY
Paul Harper
author of *Reinventing the Financial Advice Profession*

Paul's book charts the history of the financial advice profession. With decades of recruitment experience in this sector, he wanted to tell the story of the industry from the era of 'the man from the Pru' to the regulation of the industry and share what the future may hold. He published his book in 2022.

One of Paul's biggest successes to date, as well as becoming an Amazon bestseller when it launched, was being one of the finalists in the Business Book Awards in 2023 in the category of Specialist Business Book.

When I recently spoke to Paul, he told me how his book gives him great street cred and has hugely raised his profile. He often sends out a copy as a lead magnet as it helps him to cement the relationship with potential clients. And people can buy a copy and check him out before they engage his company's services.

Reach out to book clubs

Reach out to book clubs or reading groups that align with your book's genre or theme. Offer to provide author interviews or participate in discussions about your book. You'll hear from Zana Goic Petricevic in the next chapter who has used this strategy for her first book.

Arrange book signings

Arrange book signings at local bookstores, libraries, or community events. Engage with readers, sign copies of your book, and use the opportunity to connect with potential fans. You will hear from Zoe Dronfield in the next chapter who is exploring this as one of her strategies.

Write your next book

Finally, a great way to continue to get noticed is by writing another book! If it's not too late, think about this from the beginning. You may have a sequence of books that follow a particular theme, like a series of 'How to' guides. Or your books may simply show a sequence of progression. Or you may have similar books for different audiences.

After writing and publishing my first book, I said never again. Eighteen months later I launched my second, and now I have ten to my name! Although I have already shared snippets, here is a comprehensive overview of how I did it and no, I didn't think about this from the beginning!

My first book, *The Secrets of Successful Coaches* (March 2011), based on my NLP Master Practitioner project, explored the mindset behind successful coaching businesses. Interviewing coaches in the UK and US, I applied their insights to transform my own business.

How to Stand Out in your Business (November 2012) shared the results of implementing the principles from my first book, offering a process to help clients stand out in their businesses.

Your Book is the Hook (March 2015) was driven by clients who started asking for guidance on writing their own books. I discovered my talent for helping authors to find their best idea and to structure their book effectively. This led to my book mentoring services and the publication of my third book.

The Mouse That Roars (February 2016) was developed after completing a project called 'A Year to Live'. A personal journey, this book reveals how a shy child became an accidental entrepreneur through coaching and transformative experiences.

The first edition of *Book Marketing Made Simple* (April 2017) expanded the book marketing part of *Your Book is the Hook*, focusing on effective book marketing strategies at all stages of a book's creation, helping authors avoid common pitfalls.

Becoming An Authority (October 2019) was originally an audiobook experiment, and it highlighted clients' stories and case studies, emphasising writing as a means to establish authority and credibility.

The *Business Book Planner* and the *Book Writing Journal* (January 2021) were created as practical resources to guide authors through the writing process and provide space for notes and ideas.

Then *The 7 Shifts* (May 2022) was developed initially as a lead magnet, setting the stage for successful book writing by preparing readers to refine their ideas, share their stories, and establish a clear framework.

And, of course, in 2023, I have created a second edition of this book as well as the *Book Marketing Planner,* and there are a couple of others bubbling away in the background!

 **THINGS TO THINK ABOUT**

I'm sure that you've got plenty of ideas to continue to promote your book. I'd love to hear about them. Feel free to email karen@librotas.com to tell me what they are.

Be innovative, partner with like-minded individuals, and never stop shouting about your book.

I hope that the real-life examples from my clients' stories have inspired you to write, publish, and promote your book – or books!

You don't have to stop at one book. Many of my clients have plans for two, three or ten books, and actually having more books to your name is a great way not to be a one-hit wonder!

Before you move on to the final chapter, take a moment to note what you've learnt from this section. How are you going to continue to market your book after you've launched it?

_____

_____

_____

_____

_____

CHAPTER 22
Master your marketing

Your book is the hook that will get you noticed, but its ongoing promotion and marketing is the thing that will help you increase its longevity.

In this final chapter, I will explore how you can create your book marketing plan and become an authority. This will allow you to make a bigger impact in the world, leave a legacy, and build your business further. I will share three client stories so you can see how the material in this book can work in practice.

Create your book marketing plan

When I interviewed Duncan Brodie for my first book, he gave me one piece of advice which has stuck with me some 14+ years later. He said focus on three forms of marketing and do them well. I do believe that once you've nailed these three things and got the systems in place, you can consider introducing more strategies to have a multi-pronged approach to your marketing. When considering which forms of marketing to implement, consider your type of business, your ideal reader, and where you can reach them. Also be mindful of your preferred approach and where you get results.

As I mentioned in the beginning, it's never too early to start marketing your book, and be mindful that the way you market your book in the initial stages will evolve as you approach the launch. Building your community and nurturing your contacts will be key in the early stages and you are likely to ramp up this promotion as you approach your launch.

Importantly, never stop talking about your book. Remember, every conversation you have with someone about your book is a form of marketing! And when you are smart about the process of marketing your book, you will also multipurpose the content that you create, so that all the information you produce supports the development and growth of your business.

When you create your book marketing plan, look at the success stories shared in this book to see what is truly possible. You can go to www.librotas.com/free for a downloadable marketing plan that you can complete with your ideas and actions.

In terms of success, let me remind you to consider what this means to you. It may not be simply about how many books you sell. It is likely to also come from the lives you impact, the difference you make, and how your book allows you to be on purpose every day.

Of course you'll want to recoup your investment, so focus on the opportunities you want to come off the back of your book, whether this is from clients, speaking engagements, product sales, or other lucky breaks that you may never have imagined before you published your book.

Also, don't try and do everything yourself. My business wouldn't be where it is today if I didn't have trainers, coaches, and mentors who have taught me so much, alongside a team who help with strategy, processes, and tech to enable the business to operate in a seamless way. Embrace the tools available to you and those who can help you to achieve success.

Become an authority

Becoming an authority is a critical aspect of book marketing that is often overlooked. Your book, when written well, automatically establishes you as an authority and showcases your knowledge and wisdom. It differentiates you from your competitors and positions you as an expert in your field.

Think of your book as more than just a product to sell. It can serve as a tool to attract clients, gain publicity, and open doors to new opportunities. When you're aligned with your message and embody what you teach, it becomes easier to show up in a bigger way.

Let me start to wrap up by sharing some real-life success stories of authors who used their books to firmly step into their authority and make a bigger impact.

CLIENT STORY
Zana Goic Petricevic
author of *Bold Reinvented*

I've had the pleasure of working with Zana since March 2020 when she originally approached me to support her to write her first book. During this period, I've seen Zana truly step into her authority. Originally a coach and trainer operating in her home country of Croatia, she decided to write her book in her second language of English to create a global business.

In May 2023, when I asked Zana to tell me what she has achieved since writing and publishing her first book (and she is currently working on her second), this is what she told me:

"I have developed my speaking business off the back of my book and have been invited to speak at conferences and in-house speaking events for big global clients in professional industry services across the world. I most recently did a keynote to regional leaders from the pharma industry and they all got a copy of the book, which resulted in wonderful feedback.

"My leadership development business increased as I became known as the authority for bold leadership and was asked to do a number of programmes on that again globally. I was asked to do the APAC (Asia and Pacific) tour where I spoke in India, Japan, China and Asia within a two-week period to encourage participants to take risks and lead boldly. I am currently expanding my authority to bold leadership for women leaders, and I am being hired by big companies such as TikTok.

"I've been told that my book is on the agenda of many book clubs and one of them is the IE Business School Alumni book club that invited me to moderate a discussion on my own book. I am preparing the coaching programme based on the model from my book and have created a 1:1 coaching package based on it.

"My revenues doubled in 2022 vs 2021, and my revenues for the first 5 months of this year are already at 70% of my total revenues in 2022.

"I think I can say now with full confidence that I am not only the authority in bold leadership, but I've actually created a brand out of myself. And I'm noticing I'm owning that brand more and more as I come up on the stage – with full authenticity and no worries if everyone will like me. I like what I stand for and that does not have to be everyone's cup of tea. Still, judging by the revenue increase, it seems I'm doing just fine!"

I am currently supporting Zana with her second book!

CLIENT STORY
Zoe Dronfield
author of *Mind Over Manipulators*

Before Zoe Dronfield wrote and launched her book, she was already in the public eye. Her book is memoir in style, documenting her journey of recovery after being tortured and almost murdered, sharing red flags to support others who are facing a similar experience. When I asked her to tell me about her successes to date after publishing her book in March 2022, this is what she told me:

"Many people know about my story. It was originally reported in the *Daily Mail* newspaper, before being picked up by other news outlets countrywide. I'm well known in Coventry, and over the years, I have appeared on BBC News, ITV News, Sky News, and I'm often sought after as the voice for those who suffer from abuse in the UK.

"At the moment, I've been actively promoting my book on the radio, leveraging the opportunity to ask for clips that not only promote my book but also give exposure to the radio station and raise my profile. I'm currently in discussions with my local Waterstones for a potential book-signing event, and I'm excited about the prospect.

"Additionally, I've noticed that people often find my story online and visit my website to learn more about where I have been featured, which further elevates my profile. As a result of my book, I have received invitations to talk at various events and conferences. When I speak at events for the police and domestic abuse charities, I'm always pleased to see queues of people eager to get a copy of my book.

"Perhaps the most exciting development recently was my trip to Los Angeles, where I had the opportunity to meet with a friend and advocate. During our discussions, we explored the potential for a Netflix documentary pitch. Whilst it's still in the early stages, it's an exciting possibility to keep an eye on!

"These experiences illustrate how my book has been instrumental in raising my profile, attracting opportunities, and allowing me to make a bigger impact with my message."

CLIENT STORY
Sarah Hamilton-Gill FCIPD
author of *Leap into HR Consulting*

Sarah wrote *Leap into HR Consulting* in 2020, when COVID-19 forced her to change her business overnight. And over the last few years, her book has had some amazing results. This is what she shared with me in May 2023.

"I've sold over 1000 books on Amazon alone, resulting in £10k of passive income – pure profit. And this doesn't take into account the books I have gifted to those who have joined my HR Consultants bootcamp or through other retail outlets.

"My book has been instrumental in introducing readers to my unique process and approach in the field of HR consulting. Many of them have signed up to work with me through my bootcamp, which provides comprehensive support for setting up their own HR consulting business. To date, I've supported over 135 clients through the bootcamp, and I have coached many more on a one-to-one basis and through my retreat in Corfu.

"What has led to my success? It's a combination of spotting a niche, consistently showing up, and putting in the effort. As mentioned in an earlier chapter, webinars have been an effective strategy for attracting new leads and engaging with my audience.

"In addition to webinars, I launched my podcast in May 2021, which currently reaches over 1000 monthly listeners across 50 countries, and I'm about to increase the frequency of episodes from once a fortnight to once a week.

"Lately, I've been dedicating my efforts to breaking into the US market. Ten of my bootcamp clients are based in America, and they've been spreading the word about my programme among their colleagues and networks.

"To generate traction, I've found success with Facebook Ads and Amazon Ads. However, I must highlight that LinkedIn has been an incredibly powerful tool for networking and building valuable professional connections.

"I'm proud to share that my book is now an accredited book in the Society for Human Resource Management (SHRM) book library in the US so members can gain CPD (Continued Professional Development) hours by reading and completing assessments based on my book.

"Recently, I had the incredible opportunity to be interviewed on US TV, with the segment also due to stream in China, India, and through social media platforms, reaching viewers worldwide.

"And my marketing journey is far from over. I have exciting plans in store, including the creation of a second edition for my current book and the development of a new book to extend my impact and reach."

Simply show up

Whilst writing a book is a significant accomplishment, continuing to build your authority requires bravery, courage, and a willingness to show up in a bigger way. Enhance your online presence, share valuable content, and seize opportunities aligned with your goals and values.

Be amazing. Be real and authentic. And be you.

Step out with confidence, show up in a bigger way, and use your book to reach more people and make a significant difference in the world.

And if I can help you further, please reach out to me at karen@librotas.com. Whether you are thinking about your book or further down the line, then let's chat further about how I might be able to support you.

Next steps

You can download additional resources at www.librotas.com/free including some of the links and information I've included in this book.

When I finished writing this book, I realised that there was so much more I could include, but I had to stop somewhere. So please do sign up for my free newsletter and blogs at www.librotas.com, so that you can keep up to date with new information and articles that will evolve from writing this book.

You can also find out more about how I work at www.librotas.com, including our Smart Author System programme, writing retreats, and other events that may interest you. And if you'd like my personal support in any part of the book writing, publishing, and promotion process, then drop me a line.

Please keep in touch and I'd love to know the results that you've got from reading this book and implementing my suggestions. Oh and please do leave a review on Amazon!

You can email me at karen@librotas.com or contact me via my website. I look forward to hearing from you.

Contributors to this book

Steve Bimpson, HoneyBee Marketing
www.joinedup-marketing.com

Ginny Carter, Marketing Twentyone
www.marketingtwentyone.co.uk

Steve Randall, Communication Generation
www.cgpods.com

Alison Colley, Real Employment Law Advice
www.realemploymentlawadvice.co.uk

Alice Fewings, Alice Fewings LinkedIn Trainer and Coach
www.alicefewings.com

Karen Duncan, Pony Pony Pony
www.ponyponypony.co.uk

Caroline Andrew-Johnstone, The Networking Rebel
and MD of 4Networking
www.4nonline.biz

Ellen Watts, Ellen Unlimited
www.ellen-unlimited.com

Paul Newton, Mental Theft
www.mentaltheft.co.uk

Helen McCusker, Book Publicist
Twitter: @helenmccusker or Instagram: @book_publicist

Samantha Pearce, SWATT Books
www.swatt-books.co.uk

Elliott Frisby, MonkeyNut Audiobooks
www.monkeynutuk.com

Dielle Hannah, Igloo Studios
www.igloomusic.co.uk

Naomi Jane Johnson, Digital Creator
www.naomijanejohnson.co.uk

Client stories

Jenny Phillips, Inspired Nutrition
www.inspirednutrition.co.uk

Rochelle Bugg, Creative Copywriter
www.rochellebugg.com

Helen Monaghan, HM Coaching
www.hmcoaching.co.uk

Joanna Gaudoin, Inside Out Image
www.insideoutimage.co.uk

Sheryl Andrews, Step by Step Listening
www.stepbysteplistening.com

Lorraine Palmer, Healthy Eating Specialist
www.lorrainepalmer.com

Sally Kay, Reflexology Lymph Drainage
www.reflexologylymphdrainage.co.uk

Della Judd, Executive Coach and Consultant
www.dellajudd.co.uk

Kate Barrett, eFocus Marketing
www.e-focusmarketing.com

Nick Fewings, Ngagement Works
www.ngagementworks.com

Gina Visram, Limitless Coaching
www.limitlesscoaching.com

Louise Evans, The 5 Chairs
www.the5chairs.com

Zana Goic Petricevic, Bold Leadership Culture
www.boldleadership-culture.com

James Morehen, Morehen Performance
www.morehenperformance.com

Sarah Hamilton-Gill FCIPD, Leap into HR Consulting
www.leapintoconsulting.com

Paul Harper, Paul Harper Search
www.paulharpersearch.co.uk

Zoe Dronfield, Campaigner against injustice
www.zoedronfield.com

Emma Heptonstall, The Divorce Alchemist
www.emmaheptonstall.com

About Karen Williams

Karen Williams is The Book Mentor at Librotas® and a leading authority in helping experts, entrepreneurs, and leaders write and market non-fiction books. With a focus on sharing their stories and messages, Karen guides her clients through the entire process of planning, writing, marketing, and launching a book that boosts credibility, attracts new clients, and creates exciting opportunities.

Her journey in the business world began in January 2006 when she decided to transition from her 15-year corporate career in hospitality, human resources, and training. Seeking guidance, she hired her first coach and discovered her true calling. After training as a coach herself, she founded Self Discovery Coaching in November 2006.

Initially specialising in career coaching and offering corporate training using DISC personal profiling, Karen soon realised that to achieve success, she needed to learn from others. To further her expertise and initially as part of her NLP Master Practitioner modelling project, she conducted interviews with over 25 top performance coaches, including Michael Neill, Dawn Breslin, and Gladeana McMahon in 2009.

The valuable insights gained from these interviews led to Karen's first book, *The Secrets of Successful Coaches*, which became an Amazon bestseller in 2011. This achievement was swiftly followed by her second bestseller, *How to Stand Out in your Business*, published in 2012.

In 2014, she published *Your Book is the Hook* as she rebranded herself as The Book Mentor, marking a significant evolution in her business. Her fourth book, *The Mouse That Roars*, published in 2015, inspired her TEDx Talk of the same name.

Book Marketing Made Simple was initially published in June 2017 and has undergone significant updates for this second edition in 2023. Karen has also authored five more successful books: *Becoming An Authority*, *Business Book Planner*, *Book Writing Journal*, *The 7 Shifts*, and *Book Marketing Planner*.

Karen excels at helping individuals clarify their ideas, create a powerful structure, and develop a captivating hook for their businesses. She is passionate about empowering authors to self-validate and self-fund the writing process, emphasising the importance of marketing their book from the moment their brilliant idea takes shape.

Karen's clients receive personalised support through one-to-one and group mentoring sessions, writing retreats in Spain, and online programmes such as the Smart Author System. With the assistance of her exceptional team, Karen guides clients from the initial idea to publication, covering all aspects such as planning, writing accountability, time management, taming their inner critic, developmental reviews, editing and proofreading, design, publishing in print and e-book formats, publicity and PR.

Beyond her expertise as a book mentor, Karen also loves to speak, regularly features in the media, and occasionally does crazy things like jumping out of a plane and walking on hot coals!

To delve deeper into Karen's story, check out *The Mouse That Roars* and watch her inspiring TEDx Talk recorded in October 2017. In December 2017, Karen received the Maximise Creative Business of the Year Award and has been featured in prominent publications, media and podcasts including the *Daily Mail*, the *Daily Express*, BBC Radio, *Coach Magazine*, and the Sharkpreneur podcast. Karen is also a Partner Member of the Alliance of Independent Authors (ALLi).

Contact Karen

Find out more about Karen and her work at www.librotas.com and you can email karen@librotas.com.

You can also follow Karen on the following platforms:

Facebook: www.facebook.com/librotas
Twitter: www.twitter.com/librotas
LinkedIn: www.linkedin.com/in/karenwilliamslibrotas
YouTube: www.youtube.com/@librotas

Endnotes

1   www.thesocialshepherd.com/blog/twitter-statistics
2   https://news.linkedin.com/about-us#Statistics
3   https://foundationinc.co/lab/b2b-marketing-linkedin-stats/
4   https://blog.hubspot.com/blog/tabid/6307/bid/30030/
    linkedin-277-more-effective-for-lead-generation-than-
    facebook-twitter-new-data.aspx
5   https://thesocialshepherd.com/blog/instagram-statistics
6   www.newdigitalage.co/retail/why-amazon-has-become-the-
    driving-force-in-the-growth-of-ecommerce
7   www.insiderintelligence.com/content/
    looking-for-a-new-product-you-probably-searched-amazon

Printed in Great Britain
by Amazon

28513547R00159